Crystals
Strong and Beautiful

By
Lettie Vantol

Photographs by Ute Sonnenberg &
Kathy Tompsett

Order this book online at www.trafford.com/06-1280
or email orders@trafford.com

Most Trafford titles are also available at major online book retailers.

© Copyright 2007 Lettie Vantol.

All rights reserved. No part of this publication may be reproduced, stored in a retrieval system, or transmitted, in any form or by any means, electronic, mechanical, photocopying, recording, or otherwise, without the written prior permission of the author.

Note for Librarians: A cataloguing record for this book is available from Library and Archives Canada at www.collectionscanada.ca/amicus/index-e.html

Printed in Victoria, BC, Canada.

ISBN: 978-1-4120-9525-9

We at Trafford believe that it is the responsibility of us all, as both individuals and corporations, to make choices that are environmentally and socially sound. You, in turn, are supporting this responsible conduct each time you purchase a Trafford book, or make use of our publishing services. To find out how you are helping, please visit www.trafford.com/responsiblepublishing.html

Our mission is to efficiently provide the world's finest, most comprehensive book publishing service, enabling every author to experience success. To find out how to publish your book, your way, and have it available worldwide, visit us online at www.trafford.com/10510

Trafford PUBLISHING®

www.trafford.com

North America & international
toll-free: 1 888 232 4444 (USA & Canada)
phone: 250 383 6864 ♦ fax: 250 383 6804
email: info@trafford.com

The United Kingdom & Europe
phone: +44 (0)1865 487 395 ♦ local rate: 0845 230 9601
facsimile: +44 (0)1865 481 507 ♦ email: info.uk@trafford.com

Disclaimer: This book is not intended in any way to be interpreted as prescribing for any illness or other physical and/or mental conditions.

This book is dedicated to my very dear friend Carolyn Ryan without whose support and encouragement this book would not have seen the light of day.

Crystals are:

Clear transparent ice-like minerals, especially pure Quartz
   (Oxford dictionary)

A homogenous solid, formed by a repeating three dimensional pattern of atoms, ions, or molecules and having fixed distances between constituent parts
   (American Heritage College)

A mineral, especially a transparent form of quartz, having a crystalline structure, often characterised by external planar faces
   (Anon)

A natural or synthetic crystalline material having piezoelectric or semi-conducting properties
   (Anon)

INTRODUCTION

I am delighted to write a foreword for this informative book on crystals and healing. The book is meant as a general understanding of crystals and is written in a friendly, personal and easy to understand manner, which makes it unique. Rather than equating crystals to physical symptoms, Lettie offers a more sensible and workable approach and underlines that this is a complementary therapy and not an alternative. The accent on crystal healing is not on physical symptoms only, because it is holistic and addresses the causes of illness.

Lettie has many years of experience in crystal healing as well as many other forms of complementary medicine. As a teacher, apart from being highly spiritual and easygoing, she has an excellent understanding of students' needs. She also comes from a point where healing is a way of life rather than a 9 to 5 job and underlines that it can be a challenging journey which usually demands many life changes and therefore will take time.

I wholeheartedly recommend this book and trust that many people new to crystals, as well as those more familiar, will gain a greater understanding of how crystals work and can contribute to our lives and help in a practical way.

Henriette Maasdijk
Principal of the Vibrational Healing Foundation London

CRYSTALS STRONG AND BEAUTIFUL

Page 9 WHY ANOTHER BOOK
Page 15 MY PERSONAL CRYSTAL JOURNEY

Page 27   1. HEALING WITH CRYSTALS
1) Introduction To Crystal Therapy
2) Ancient, Mediaeval & Modern History Of Crystals
3) The Transformative Power Of Crystals

Page 63   2. CRYSTAL BASICS FOR PERSONAL USE
1) How Do Crystals Heal
2) Choosing Crystals
3) Cleansing Crystals
4) Programming Crystals

Page 101   3. CRYSTALS AS A MYTH
1) The Mystical Pendulum
2) Crystals And Religion
3) Crystals And Astrology

Page 125   4. SHARPEN YOUR SENSES
1) Energy Awareness
2) Seeing Energy
3) Sensing Crystals

Page 149   5. USING CRYSTAL POWER
1) Protection With Crystals
2) Crystal Mandalas
3) Crystals And Meditation
4) First Aid With Crystals
5) Animals And Crystals

Page 201   6. THE SECRET MISSION OF CRYSTALS
1) The Crystals' Soul Journey
2) The Earthkeepers
3) The Crystal Skulls

Page 235   7. EXPOSE YOUR SENSES TO CRYSTAL THERAPY
Experiencing And Finding A Crystal Therapy Treatment

WHY ANOTHER BOOK

WHY ANOTHER BOOK

Many books have already been written about crystals, so why is another book on crystals needed? On close scrutiny you will find that most of these books have a very similar theme, covering mainly information regarding individual properties of crystals, what they mean, how to choose, clean and (always!) how to discover your personal birthstone. All of this is very important, but in this book, I would suggest that you view crystals and their properties from a different perspective. Having 'lived' crystals for well over twenty years, as well as teaching crystal therapy for over fourteen years, I would like to share some of my personal experiences with crystals. Be forewarned: you may find these somewhat unusual!

Having introduced hundreds of students to Crystal Healing, one fact has become clear. Not only do the crystals have a healing effect, but there are subtle personal changes which take place in students and therapists when working closely with crystals. I have personally witnessed this phenomenon again and again. In addition to regaining wellness in the physical body, it has been amazing to observe how crystals can positively affect spiritual growth. These transformational effects, which crystals often bring about, are seldom acknowledged and deserve mentioning. My experience is that these changes usually occur when working with crystals with an attitude of respect, knowledge, integrity and conscious intent; and it has been a great joy to see this happening in many of my students whilst they attend the crystal therapy course.

Crystals are very powerful tools and their energy has the capacity to bring about remarkable 'wake-up-calls'. From the moment anybody sincerely starts working with crystals, changes happen! It almost appears as if certain crystals have been waiting in the wings to jump in at the appropriate time to assist the student on the evolutionary path in the most subtle and imaginative ways.

In this book, I am encouraging you to open your awareness to some lesser-known methods of working with crystals, which may affect **your** life in a positive way, as well as that of other people and the environment! Living in this time of great change on both global and personal levels requires adaptation to adjust to this 'new' world. In spite of the daily disasters we see on T.V. and read in newspapers, it is important to remain positive and confident that the eventual outcome of this change will be a better and more caring world - but first we have to get there! Meantime, each of us can contribute much in our own individual way to accelerate the process for good. You do not necessarily have to be a therapist to do this. Each of us can contribute so much in our individual way; be it by sending out healing thoughts to people and animals or by helping the environment on an energetic or practical level. When we send out these thoughts with the help of the crystals, results may be achieved twice as quickly. It is my wish that this book will create a greater understanding of the help crystals can offer you personally in many different ways to ease your personal life's journey. Having been fortunate to observe this at first hand in my students, I know it works!

MY PERSONAL CRYSTAL JOURNEY

MY PERSONAL CRYSTAL JOURNEY

Crystals have held a fascination for me as long as I can remember!

Born in Holland, I was the eldest of eleven children. Ours was a very busy and rombustious household although Dad ruled his roost like a sergeant major and ran it (as far as it was in his power!) like a military establishment. From necessity my mother was a great believer in 'delegating' household tasks, whatever our age, be it dusting, washing up (prior to the dish-washer age!) or peeling a large pan of potatoes for the next day.

By the time I reached the ripe age of nine, I was an 'expert' at looking after younger siblings. Needless to say my talents were in great demand, especially during school holidays when I would often be put in charge of four or five of the younger ones. On sunny days we would walk the three miles to the local swimming pool, our rucksacks bursting with healthy picnics (not to be eaten before reaching the pool!). Keeping this little group in tow was more than a handful for a nine year old! The twin brothers in particular had very original minds when it came to mischief and the big-sister discipline was sorely needed to keep them on the straight and narrow and to get them to our destination and back in one piece.

There were similar outings over the years, but the highlight was the local park. It had lovely paths strewn with the most beautiful gravel! Having pushed the pram with the latest toddler, sandwiches, peanuts and lemonade, and several siblings in tow, we would bag a bench in the play area and make it our home for the day. The youngsters would happily play in the sandpit and I would hover at the edge where the shiny gravel was. While keeping half an eye on the youngsters, I would fill yet another cigar box with the most beautiful of these treasures. In those far-off days the sun always shone brightly, highlighting the beauty of my 'gems' and in spite of my 'responsibilities' these gorgeous looking stones made these trips very worthwhile. Mysteriously though, the cigar boxes with my treasures kept disappearing, later to be found empty... Vaguely, the boys were blamed, but it was not until much later that I suspected my mother had emptied them on our gravel path in the garden!

Our family was of 'solid' Catholic stock and churchgoing was not just a weekly, but rather a daily practice, which was often the cause of many a feigned tummy ache for us children. Both our parents were psychic, and natural healers, and we normally adhered strictly to the 'proper church' rules. Looking back, and aware of the church's views on healing in the thirties and forties of the past century, I often wondered how my parents coped with this moral dilemma. It must have been mother's no nonsense 'God-is-not-a pea-counter' philosophy (her favourite expression) which permitted her to carry on with healing while travelling this earthly journey. Although the time was not ripe to practice this openly, it was the most normal thing for us children to have a healing hand put on a painful spot or aching tooth 'to make it better'. The exception was with the boys; when they were hurt in a fight they were often left to suffer to learn their lessons! I wonder if ever they did.

Since all this domesticity did not do much for my schoolwork, my parents sent me away to boarding school when I was eleven, where the routine was more conventional. Having a linguistic aptitude, I specialised in languages and at the age of nineteen spent some time in Switzerland as au pair to improve my fluency in French. After some rather unexciting office jobs back in Holland I came to England when I was twenty-three. England had always fascinated me. While at school, geography was my favourite subject and nothing was more exciting than studying the map of England, because I already knew I would go there when I would be a grown-up!

After a variety of jobs, marriage followed and my two daughters were born. Finances were tight and our budget badly needed some topping up. With two small children to care for it was very difficult to find a suitable job. After doing some bits of office work and translations at home, which did not really improve my household finances, I eventually started my own business working from home, which I ran for twenty years and supported us all. This business involved moving zoo animals to destinations all over the world.

As my enterprise grew, travelling was an integral part of my job. This included visiting clients abroad and attending conferences. This became easier as the girls got older. Amazingly, it was during this period in my life that my path crossed many people in need of healing. The animals in my care needed healing as well. I spent many hours roughing it in large cargo aircrafts, accompanying my charges while talking to them and sending healing. (Somehow Zebras, being notoriously nervous animals, responded well.) Thus, healing became part of my life. During these travelling years, while visiting major zoos overseas, I occasionally had the opportunity to spend some time in the cities I visited. The best part was finding and visiting those alluring crystal shops….and so it started!

By the time my girls finished their education, healing had become a major part of my life. Although never instructed, my hands would know where to go during healing sessions and I would use pressure on certain points, which alleviated the condition. Later I learned that these were appropriate acupoints (points used by acupuncturists located all over the body), which led me to suspect I must have been an acupuncturist in a past life. Clearly, the time had come to make my healing work official!

A friend told me about a Kinesiology course, which was the first therapy instruction that I received. This was followed by Reflexology,

Massage, Aromatherapy, Lymph drainage, Cranio Sacral and a variety of advanced massage courses. From necessity, I still had my business and left my assistant in the office while attending classes to learn yet another therapy. In the end, all these hard earned pieces of paper finally made my healing therapy 'legal'!

Now, suitably qualified, the time had come to start a practice. I rented a room for two days a week from my acupuncturist friend, Stephen, who had a practice in Surrey (still leaving my assistant in charge while I made less money than I paid her). It was a start. Slowly the practice built up, but the income was not sufficient to sustain a modest living without my business, although I was ready to let that go....

Some of my close friends suggested that in addition to the therapies I should do some teaching. But this was 1989 and complementary therapies were not yet 'in'. However, I felt I had to do this. I hastily embarked on a teaching course and subsequently contacted my local Adult Education College, where they were surprisingly open to the idea of teaching complementary therapies. The college happened to be looking for some new courses that might appeal to the students of the day. Luckily for me at this particular time, Aromatherapy and Reflexology were just becoming better known and a lot of publicity was given to these new therapies. Thus accepted, my teaching career was launched.

Meantime, I had already collected many crystals. Their attraction was based purely on their beauty – or so I believed! Then a strange thing happened. A friend gave me a very special crystal and, WOW! I could not believe the energy this crystal radiated. I felt its energy travelling throughout my body. I could not put it down. Then I remembered the crystals I had collected from different parts of the world and decided to 'experiment'.

I started with relaxation and meditation while holding the various individual crystals and simply 'sensed'. It was a revelation! I started making notes of the specific feelings and energy each one radiated. It was inconceivable that I had not been aware of this sooner. I needed to make up for lost time.

As time passed I persevered with this practice. As I was holding crystals during meditation, slowly bits of information started to filter through and over time healing patterns were created, i.e. ways of applying crystals to bring about transformation on the physical level.

One of my first experiences brought relief from the severe migraines I had been suffering over many years. Not only did I learn the origin of this debilitating condition that had plagued me for so long, but also how to safely use specific crystals on certain points of the body (acupoints) for actual pain relief.

At the time, few books on the healing aspects of crystals were available, and I absorbed them all. One of the first books that inspired me was by Mellie Uyldert[1]. It is practical and down to earth. It has a mass of information and interesting stories, originally written in Dutch, but later translated into English. Other books by Gurudas[2] and Kozminsky[3] are full of interesting facts and information and are still very worth while reading today. Later I discovered Katrina Raphaell's books and was pleasantly surprised that many of her experiences on crystals coincided with the information I had received. A vast number of books have been published since, but these 'oldies' still offer a tremendous amount of information (These can still be obtained today, especially in older specialist bookshops – although often second hand)

Soon I learned which books 'felt true', as well as those that 'did not'. I managed to attend some basic workshops in the United States and also in France where I hoped to learn something more valuable than that which came from my nebulous source. However, I soon found that the 'direct information' that came through my meditations was a lot more helpful to me than course work. My enthusiasm grew by the day. It was exciting to learn that crystals can transform us on the spiritual and the emotional level as well as the

---

1 The Magic of Precious Stones. Turnstone Press 1981, ISBN 0-85030-798-8
2 Gem Elixirs & Vibrational Healing, Cassandra Press 1989, ISBN 0-961-58750-4
3 Isidore Kozminsky. The magic & Science of Jewels & Stones, Cassandra Press. ISBN 0-9615875

physical level. This information from my meditations superseded all the other therapies I had learned and practised. I simply had to share this in my classes (aromatherapy and reflexology), in talks with colleagues, patients, friends and anyone who would listen! It was not long before I started giving talks left, right and centre. Meanwhile, I practised on everyone willing, with amazingly positive results.

No doubt fed up to the teeth listening to me, my friends suggested I should teach crystal healing, after all, I taught other complementary therapies. Splendid idea! I approached the college where I had spent many years learning other therapies, but they decided it was too way-out. Apparently nobody wanted to know.... or so it seemed.

Having a strong feeling that teaching crystals was my life's path, I meditated on it and received the definite message from several sources to start my own school. Well, I started my business from scratch, so why not a school? Thus, the Vantol College of Crystal Therapy was born in 1992.

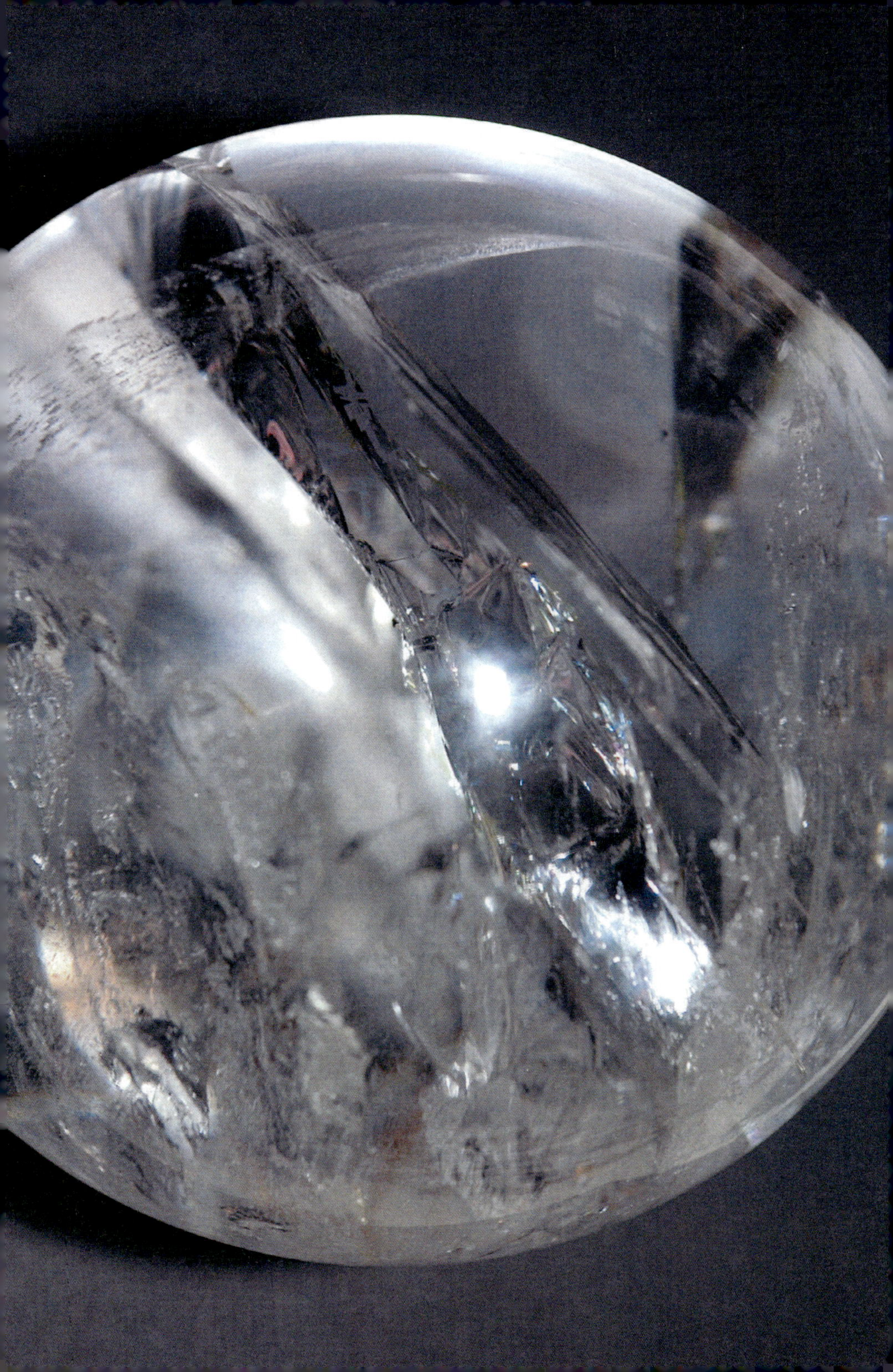

Clear Quartz Sphere

HEALING WITH CRYSTALS

INTRODUCTION TO CRYSTAL THERAPY

WHAT MAKES A PERSON TAKE UP CRYSTAL HEALING?

There are many ways in which people are drawn to Crystal Healing, an apparently 'new' therapy. As humanity is becoming increasingly sensitive, many more people are open to the energy of crystals and intuitively know they can be applied for healing the human energy system. I believe this often happens when people have worked with crystals in a similar capacity in previous incarnations. It also happens that people, already established in one or another healing module or energy therapy, desire to extend their treatment range by taking up Crystal Therapy. Sensitive nurses quite often join our courses because they would like to extend their healing skills to further help their patients.

Quite often people join a crystal healing course without any previous knowledge of the subject whatsoever. What they all have in common is a strong love for, and attraction to, crystals. In addition, they have a feeling that they seriously want to learn more about healing to help others and work with these 'special beings'. As I consider crystals to be a life form to be respected, I call them 'beings'. Students intuitively know that a course with the words 'crystal' and 'healing' in it could provide answers, perhaps even to subconscious questions.

It is as though the crystals themselves step in to entice the student to find out more. The most amazing thing about students attending our crystal therapy course is that, in the process of learning and working with crystals, unexpected energies are set into motion and the students discover an entirely new world. Students start to blossom and their intuition becomes very acute. I hear students say that they suddenly realise this is what they wanted to do all along.

My students tell me of memories of years past that have just surfaced that help them come to this realization. Some have mentioned collecting precious pebbles on the beach as a child, or memories that are connected with gifts of a simple crystal which was greatly treasured. I believe that on a subconscious level, and unbeknown to the student, a crystal connection had been set up several life times ago and came to fruition at the perfect time in this life.

Later on, in the process of working with crystals, these same students might well have flash-backs during treatments or meditation, revealing how they had worked with crystals and healing in a previous incarnation. During my fourteen years of teaching Crystal Therapy, it has been my privilege to observe students when they realised that they had worked together as a group in a past incarnation, and now once again are studying crystal healing together. These occasions are always an amazing and happy experience, both for the students and me. I strongly believe that there is no such thing as 'coincidence' and the amazing fact that these people were drawn to this particular course is not an exception.

Transformative Power of Crystals

As well as learning to enhance physical well-being for others, working closely with the healing energy of crystals accelerates one's personal spiritual development. Whether we know it or not, we all have agreed to attempt to learn certain things in this lifetime.

Some call this the soul contract. It is a lesser-known fact that when embarking on a serious crystal healing course certain experiences needed for the soul contract are speeded up. These students may progress at a faster rate than would have been the case without the practical hands-on work in the crystal course. Although a challenge at the time, is not the opportunity of becoming a purer healing channel, worthwhile?

To illustrate this I would like to share the following: Many students, who come to my courses, are working in a successful professional job in a commercial environment. As they progress in the two year professional course, subtle changes take place within them. This results in an awareness that their well paid job no longer holds the importance it once did. Their aspirations are shifting. They feel that playing a part in helping and healing others is really what they would like to do, preferably with the assistance of the Crystal Kingdom.

Although not always easy, life-changing decisions often are made and these students have the courage to follow a new direction. This could take the form of a new job, or changing their working environment in some way. They subsequently find that, after this major resolution, the pieces start to fall together like a perfect jigsaw and a positive transformation takes place with the help of the crystals.

Challenges during these periods of change are true opportunities for growth. Let's be honest, most of us shrink when awareness of a new 'challenge' appears on the horizon! It is at such times that we might feel the need for support, which for our students is often supplied by their peer group. It is important to remember that as well as being catalysts, crystals can, and are happy to, assist us. As catalysts, they help to draw a particular experience to us and when this learning situation is presented, they assist us in many ways.

Each of us goes through particularly memorable periods of growth or change many times in the course of our life. Some are more challenging than others, but most of us can call on the support of our human associates when faced with certain growth challenges during a particularly difficult patch. But there is more help available! As lovers of the crystal kingdom we know we can call on our crystalline friends. If only we let them, they are happy to take on the role of Personal Assistant. Our crystals are ready to sustain us with their energy on an emotional, mental and physical level.

There are many ways in which we can call upon crystals for assistance. Students of crystal healing, and those already established as crystal healers/therapists, know how to access the right crystals to receive maximum help. However, it is important to remember that their assistance is not limited to the experts. You, the reader, can turn to crystals for Self Help. You will find quite a few useful techniques described further on in this book, which everyone can use. All the same, when you are faced with a difficult emotional or physical challenge, little can equal a crystal therapy treatment given by a qualified crystal therapist. Look for one who has been professionally trained and is qualified in a vast number of different crystal healing techniques and is able to tailor this to your individual condition. (Details of where to locate a professionally qualified therapist can be found in the addendum at the end of this book.)

Transformation at a Practical & Spiritual Level

During the past fourteen years of teaching crystal therapy, it has been my privilege to work with, and observe, a large number of students whose lives have been profoundly affected in a positive way while studying and working with crystals in the healing field. Naturally, this is not restricted to students learning this therapy in a course, but to anyone who works with crystals with integrity and pure intent. There is an obvious advantage for the student working within a group context since the energy of the group assists each student and makes the experience easier. Besides the sharing and mutual support, it keeps everyone's sense of humour alive, which is a great healing tool by itself!

To recap: all of us encounter challenges, but the healing energy of crystals is ready to support you, should you choose to call upon them. In the chapter on Choosing Crystals, you will find more information about crystals, as well as guidance in helping you to find the crystal you need at any given time. Having made your choice, you can enlist the help of your special crystal and ask for strength and stamina to support you in dealing with your specific challenge and assist you during this time of personal transformation. Everyone can benefit from working with crystals and, let's face it -- you would not be reading this book if you did not have a genuine interest in crystals!

****

ANCIENT MEDIEVAL & MODERN HISTORY OF CRYSTALS

References about the use of crystals for healing and in ceremonies have been recorded extensively in history and legends. They are difficult to ignore. With the resurgence of interest in crystals, especially in reference to healing, many people can relate a tale that tells how crystals played an important part in an ancient culture.

When going back in history we find some concrete references in the bible which is commonly known written history. The best reference to crystals is of The Israeli High Priest's Breastplate, which was adorned with twelve 'precious stones'. (Book of Exodus 39:8 : *"He made also a rational with embroidered work, according to the work of the ephod, of gold, violet, purple, and scarlet twice dyed, and fine twisted linen"*)

Which stones were on the breastplate?

Biblical scholars have been fascinated by this and there are numerous pictures of the shape of this Breastplate. To those of us with an interest in crystals, it has equal appeal, but our interest is mainly in the choice of crystals set into the Breastplate. Although much has been written about the breastplate, the crystals adorning this garment have received little attention. According to the great Jewish historian Josephus, four rows of precious stones were set upon the breastplate; three in each row. Many different versions of the inlaid crystals exist, but the most quoted ones are set out below:

High Priest's Breastplate

Ruby	Topaz	Garnet
Emerald	Sapphire	Diamond
Sard	Agate	Amethyst
Beryl	Onyx	Jasper

In general, however, the following composite is the most accepted:

Judah Sardius (Red)	Issachar Topaz (Pale green)	Zebulon Carbuncle (Deep red)
Reuben Emerald (Green)	Simeon Sapphire (Deep blue)	Gad Diamond (Transparent)
Ephraim Ligure (Dull red)	Manasseh Agate (Gray)	Benjamin Amethyst (Purple)
Dan Beryl (bluish green)	Asher Onyx (Bluish white)	Naphtali Jasper (Green)

It has been said that each of the crystals in the Breastplate was engraved with the name of one of the twelve tribes of Israel. The story goes that these crystals were especially chosen by God with the intent to share the energy of that particular crystal with the members of that individual tribe. This makes a lot of sense to those of us who are involved with crystals and aware of the energies of each individual crystal.

Lemuria

Going still further back in history we have to rely on legends. Among this vast number of myths is the one about the continent of Lemuria, believed to have existed in the region of the Pacific Ocean from 200,000 BC to 50,000 BC. Details of when or why this continent disappeared are not recorded. One of the most amazing stories told is the one where crystals were purported to literally have grown out of the soil and were actually harvested! It is said that the earth's energies were much more powerful then than they are today and thus this was possible, although hard to believe!

From the ancient Lemurian legends let us continue our journey through crystal history, relying on more legends and hear-say.... which, apart from some biblical references, is all we have to go on!

Atlantis

There are many legends and theories about the existence of the mystical continent of Atlantis. The destruction of this continent must have had a tremendous impact on the entire globe and which spawned the stories of Santorini, Heliki and the cataclysmic inundation of the Mediterranean basin. The Pillars of Hercules were breached by sea water, forming the present Mediterranean. Many cities were lost and many settlements drowned. Until more evidence becomes available, exact dates are not known, but Atlantis is believed to have existed from approximately 150,000 to 10,000 BC. Legends tell us that although initially it was a wonderfully enlightened and spiritual place, certain people became greedy for power. As time went on, sadly, crystal power was purported to have been a contributing factor in the final destruction of this great continent.

The most reliable information comes to us from the great Greek philosopher Plato, who lived in Greece circa 400 BC and was the first known person to document the story of Atlantis. Plato is said to have learned of this story from one of his ancestors, named Solon, who was a much travelled Greek lawyer living in Athens around 600 BC. During a trip to Egypt, Solon met with local priests, who told him the story of the destruction of Atlantis.

According to this source, the final demise of Atlantis took place in approximately 9,600 BC and this date is corroborated by recent scientific information on ancient climatic conditions. In the journal 'Science', September 1975, scientists at Miami University confirmed that there had been a widespread deluge at the time, which would have flooded low-lying land, such as Atlantis.

What is of interest here is how, and for which purposes, crystals were used in those ancient Atlantian days. Once again we rely heavily on legends and channelled information. These sources tell us that the Atlantians were very knowledgeable about crystals. They programmed and used them for healing, supplying light for cities and many other purposes.[4] Atlantians also knew crystals could retain information etc. In short, they were familiar with the many properties of crystals and applied this knowledge to their everyday life.

Teacher Crystals

Many Atlantian high priests or dignitaries were capable of clairvoyance, and thus aware of the forthcoming disaster. They also knew that there would come a time in the distant future when humanity would be sufficiently evolved to again use the properties of crystals in a positive way. With this in mind, they programmed a vast number of crystals with information about their healing

---

4 Vibrational Medicine by Richard Gerber M.D. Bear & Co. Santa Fe, New Mexico 87504-2860

methods and sophisticated technological expertise of the period. These special crystals were buried in many places all over the earth in order that their knowledge would be preserved for future generations.

Personally, I believe this time is now! Many of these crystals have already found their way to healers who are able to access the dormant information in these special crystals. It is nothing short of miraculous how they find their way to the right person who is able to extract this stored information. These crystals are known as 'record' crystals and usually belong to the quartz family. They can be recognised by a tiny 'pyramid', etched onto one of the 'tables'. (Natural Quartz points culminate in a six pointed termination which are called 'tables')

I personally experienced a very extraordinary way a 'record' crystal found me. It must have been fifteen years ago when I attended a workshop in the South of England. It promised to be a Complementary-Not-To-Be-Missed weekend. Alas, I discovered after an uncomfortable half an hour sitting on a hard floor, that it was the most boring workshop on which I had ever wasted time and money. The woman sitting next to me was equally fed up -- judging by her body language! After some sighs, followed by giggling about the unrealistic tiresome content, she passed me a surreptitious note, "How about escaping for a cup of coffee?" I nodded. She left quietly (bathrooms are a great excuse!). I followed a few minutes later. What a relief to get out in the fresh air! Lucky for us there was a cosy little café around the corner where we could laugh about our unfortunate choice of this particular approach to Complementary Education.

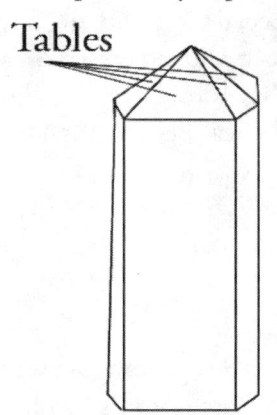

Tables

As we chatted, I found my colleague-in-misfortune was a healer and shared my interested in crystals. Suddenly, she produced a crystal out of her copious handbag, saying, "This must be for you. I had to buy this several months ago and knew I had to carry it with me to give to the right person. I now know this is you."

Having worked with crystals for sometime already, I had become accustomed to the unexpected, but I hardly knew the woman! This particular crystal was a single Madagascar quartz generator, perhaps not beautiful in the eyes of a non-crystal person, but exquisite in my eyes. After gracefully accepting this precious gift I carefully cradled it in my hands, where it fitted perfectly and where it clearly belonged! On investigating my newly acquired treasure, I found not one, but three small 'pyramids' edged onto the main table, confirming it to be a record crystal. I was so engrossed in my new gift that I missed seeing my new friend putting on her coat and hardly had time to thank her before she rushed off to catch an earlier train.

From that day to this, I have never seen this girl again, and am still amazed how this crystal found me. This special Crystal Being has been with me now for well over a decade. I have meditated with it over the years and it has supplied me with a lot of useful insight into the Crystal Kingdom as well as given me valuable healing information, which I have been able to incorporate into my teachings.

CRYSTALS AND EGYPT

While visiting the great Museum in Cairo a few years ago, I was greatly impressed by the numerous exhibits where crystals formed an important part of the display. Those around the mummified bodies are the ones I remember most. No crystal lover should miss going to a visit to this museum when visiting Egypt! After thousands of years, these crystals are still exquisite (although in great need of a good cleanse, both physically and energetically!). Amongst them are many ornate necklaces, death masks inset with the most beautiful crystals and gems of Lapis Lazuli, Malachite, Carnelian and Turquoise. These gems were considered important enough to accompany the owner on his or her eternal journey.

There is much evidence of the value the ancient Egyptians

attributed to crystals. Crystal necklaces and adornments were clearly not only considered a decoration! The Pharaohs, the High Priests, the elite and other high ranking personalities were well acquainted with the power of crystals and used them accordingly. They would not allow this power to be shared by common citizens, who duly recognised these high dignitaries to be carriers of power.

A close connection is supposed to have existed between the priesthood of Atlantis and Egypt. It was not surprising, therefore, that many of the people who are purported to have escaped from Atlantis before its destruction circa 9,600 BC migrated to Egypt. They brought with them their mystical and technical know-how, including knowledge of crystal healing. It was with this expertise and mastery of crystalline structures that they are said to have been able to build the pyramids based on the perfect Geometry of Crystals. The story goes that the great pyramid of Ghiza was topped with a giant Crystal for the purpose of capturing and utilising cosmic energies.

CRYSTALS AND THE CHINESE

When thinking of China (of course in connection with crystals) visions of Jade figurines come to mind. The Chinese have always had a great respect for Jade, which was found in abundance in this vast country. They considered it to be the 'heavenly jewel'. The great Confucius is quoted by the Chinese as having said that, 'From all time, sages have compared virtuous humanity to Jade'. During this time, it was an accepted procedure to try to prevent the body's decomposition after death. This belief led to certain emperors being buried encased in suits of interlinked jade plates to ensure that their bodies would remain intact. Sadly, recent archaeological evidence suggests that they were mistaken… but their beautiful suits remained perfectly undamaged!!

Dragons and Crystals!

The importance of crystals in the Far East can be seen in the abundance of legends and ancient folklore.

Legends that really fascinate me, and hopefully you too, are those about Crystals and Dragons. You might expect these stories to only come from China, but you would be wrong and surprised to learn that these tales also herald from South America and Europe, as well as from the Middle and Far East. Although they vary, there is a common thread running through them all. It usually involves a dragon with a large brilliant crystal, mostly a ruby, embedded in its forehead. This seems rather incongruous, but with so many narratives in a similar vein, one cannot help but wonder....

One particular legend tells about a dragon living in the cleft of certain rocks. This animal was said to have a giant ruby embedded in his forehead and this crystal radiated so much light that it would illuminate the entire valley, emphasising his presence as guardian for the local crystal mine to the people of the neighbourhood. This mine was believed to contain a vast amount of crystal treasures, similar to the superb one the dragon had on his brow. The message was clear: "Stay away! These crystals are for the dragon kingdom only!"

There are stories abound of Saints fighting dragons and in the end successfully slaying them. Staying close to home [England], there is our own Saint George who slayed the dragon, although there is no mention of a crystal.

A story is being told in the Mediterranean about a huge dragon, again with a large ruby in his head, terrorizing a large area of Southern Europe. After many prayers by the population, St. Margaret herself came down from heaven to rescue the threatened environment. She first subdued the dragon with celestial energy and subsequently removed the crystal from his forehead. Thus, the dragon lost all its power and disappeared from the valley forever. Thanks to the saint's intervention the people were liberated.

The Middle Eastern writer Sheik El Mondy wrote how a terrible dragon (again with a huge crystal in his forehead) used to terrorise the island, which was then known as Ceylon. Luckily, this tale too ended like all good stories should and a brave knight turned up to slay the beast, restoring peace to the island's inhabitants.

The fact that so many similar legends exist must convey a symbolic message. The dragon clearly represents Lower Energies. The powerful crystal in its forehead allowed the dragon to apply its brute strength to terrorise and rule his little kingdom. However, thanks to Saints and brave Knights, the Forces of Good won the day every time!

Although this is an ancient message, we recognise its moral. Today, as then, the fight for good and evil is still going on, albeit in another guise. Those of us with knowledge and interest in crystals know that they are meant to be an energy force for good. My own belief is that the Crystal Kingdom wants to work for the benefit of humankind. It is true that the crystal power can be used for either good or bad, as clearly is demonstrated in the legends of the dragons. These legendary beings, using crystals for their own empowerment, inflicted great harm and distress on their environment as well as on the crystals they used.

INDIGENOUS KNOWLEDGE

The North American Indians, being very close to nature, have always been aware of the power of these gems of Mother Earth. They knew intuitively how to harness crystal energies and shamans still use them today in their ceremonies and carry them in their medicine bundle. They also work with crystals in practical ways; by bringing the crystalline energies into their fields and gardens, where they provide valuable assistance in producing abundant crops.

Appreciation for the traditions and beliefs of the North American Indians is being rekindled at present. It makes sense, since a return to nature is of prime importance if we want to save our precious earth. I personally believe that people who spent many lifetimes as

North American Indians have at present incarnated in the Western world. They have a lot to teach us for surely relearning to connect to nature is one very important lesson. I have a friend, by profession an acupuncturist, herbalist, lecturer and earth healer, who is one of these special souls. He has an extraordinary innate knowledge of crystals, which many of us would envy, and by applying these skills in his healing work, both his patients and the environment benefits.

THE ABORIGINALS

These natives of Australia have been using crystals in their ceremonies and for healing purposes since their ancestral time, called the 'dreamtime'. They believe that crystals contain 'rainbows' which form a bridge between heaven and earth and are purported to use Amethyst for rain-making rituals.

ANCIENT PERSIA

There was a time, from approximately 6,500 to 500 BC, when vast numbers of classical scholars and priests lived in ancient Persia. Legend tells us that the most revered and worthy of the High Priests had a special quartz crystal inserted under their skin. The reason for this was two-fold: This crystal would absorb all the knowledge and wisdom this high official accumulated during his life time and secondly, it was believed that this would help him receive information from High Spiritual sources. At the death of the High Priest this crystal would, in a ceremony with great reverence, be retrieved from the corpse and inserted under the skin of his successor. This meant that all the wisdom absorbed by the crystal from its previous owner, would now be available to the current wearer. He, in turn, would add to the already vast reservoir of wisdom. Naturally, these crystals became more and more precious with each subsequent proprietor.

Ancient Greece

Great reverence was shown towards crystals in Greece as they were considered to contain Gifts from the Gods. In order that this gift would not lose any of its wonderful properties on its way from heaven to earth, it was believed that the Gods sent their light from heaven frozen in the guise of crystals. It is also the Greeks whom we have to thank for the word 'crystal', which originates from their word 'Krystallos' which means light. Crystals were greatly honoured and it was with crystals that the Greeks would light their sacrificial fires as well as the torch of their Olympic games.

The Crusades (1000 - 1200)

Knights, who went on the crusades, would return with valuable gems 'acquired' during their journey and frequently wore them as amulets because they believed them to have protective properties. Their swords and breastplates often had crystals inlaid as a sign of power and protection. The higher one's rank, the more valuable the crystals/gems that were put into their armoury!

Kings, Queens and Royalty

All over the world royalty and those in power have always possessed gems; gems being the highest and purest quality of crystals. Not only does this indicate wealth and status, but the power imparted by crystals is said to have been well known by rulers since ancient times. The famous Shah-Diamond is a perfect example of the importance and power attached by owning true crystals. It is an uncut gem in its original crystalline form. This particular Diamond was given by a Persian Ruler to his Queen in 1700 BC and this very same Diamond is still in royal possession today. In the course of many thousands of years it has actually been inscribed with three names and is very highly prized.

If we want confirmation that precious stones have always been considered evidence of power, we need only look at the ceremony of Coronation of a King or Queen. One of the most important ceremonies of the service is the placing of the golden crown, beset with precious gems, on the new ruler's head. The jewels in the crown represent the power to be bestowed on the new King or Queen. The populace at large is not, as a rule, aware of the powerful energies transmitted by the gems in the crown. Yet, way back when knowledge of energy was commonplace, people recognised the power these gems transmitted to the new monarch. They knew and acknowledged that it would help their ruler govern his or her people well.

The original selection of particular gems placed in a crown, were very carefully chosen, bearing in mind their individual vibrations. Mulling this over though, I cannot help wondering if these beautiful gems have ever been cleansed energetically....? If this is not the case, they are merely a beautiful adornment, emitting less than comfortable vibrations...

CAVE PAINTINGS

These are found in many parts of the world. Those in France and in Alta Mira in Spain were made with finely ground powdered crystal and are estimated to have been painted over 20,000 years ago and are still in good condition. Research tells us that the crushed powder was obtained from various coloured crystals found in the region. Mixed with oil it assured that the original colour would remain fresh long after the paintings dried.

CRYSTALS & HILDEGARD VON BINGEN

This is a lady whom I greatly admire! She, more than any

woman I am aware of in history, deserves a mention in this book. Hildegard von Bingen was by any account, a most remarkable lady. Born in a little place called Bermersheim in Germany in the twelfth century (1098 – 1179) she was way ahead of her time and lived in a period when women were less than second class citizens; few could either read or write. Yet, Hildegard's story is one of the most amazing ones of the Middle Ages. She was not only a truly spiritual lady, but an intellectual and accomplished in many fields. Born the tenth child of a noble family, she was at an early age given to the church and was educated by an anchoress called Jutta. As a tenth child she was a 'tithe' to God. Hildegard was very spiritual and had many visions during her lifetime. With the blessing of Pope Eugenius (1145-1153) she wrote them down and many transcripts have been translated. Not surprisingly perhaps, she was also a healer and known as a 'Mystic' in her lifetime. As a Catholic Nun she was the founder of a convent in Bingen, Germany, and in later life founded a second convent across the Rhine from Bingen.

She also was a composer of religious music and often wrote text to her songs. Several of her compositions have been revived in a modern version and are today available on CD. Hildegard was also an artist who produced beautiful embroideries, pictures of these can still be seen today. Furthermore, she was an accomplished author who wrote an amazing number of major works, many of them on religious themes in a time of great spiritual turmoil. Hildegard even wrote a moral play, which is said to have been performed by the nuns in her convent. She wrote about natural history and the healing powers of nature and natural subjects and, what endeared her most to me, wrote about the "Curative Powers of Stones (crystals)". Michael Gienger, well known for writing on crystal healing and greatly admired by crystal therapists, has recently produced a book based on Hildegard's writings on the healing properties of crystals.[5♦] This makes fascinating reading. She was very aware of both the physical and spiritual properties of crystals and goes into great details when describing their individual

---

5 Die Heilsteine der Hildegard von Bingen by Michael Gienger, Neue Erde Verlag, Saarbruecken Germany2004. To date only available in German

properties, also supplying their basic chemical composition.

In her interpretations of crystal properties she was very much influenced by the Chinese principles of dampness, air, heat, coldness, and also water. Her visions regarding the properties of the crystals themselves are very interesting and they have an amazing conformity with the conclusions our students have reached during 14 years of group sensings in our college. (Sensitivity training forms an important part of the curriculum.) Besides sensing crystals in class, students are asked to carry the stones sensed and to meditate with them. Subsequently they have to supply their personal feedback and the similarities of the outcome of this coordinated exercise over a period, are quite amazing. Comparable sensings have been carried out in Germany by Michael Gienger's group and his excellent book is published in English (translated from German)

The manner in which Hildegard applied crystals for healing is not necessarily a method we would use today, but they are nevertheless extremely interesting and I cannot leave the subject without a few quotations (tongue in cheek!):

Amethyst: *When suffering bruises or inflammation, moisten an Amethyst with your saliva and massage the affected spot. The skin will very quickly return to normal proportions*

Bloodstone (Heliotrope**)**: *Those having difficulty breathing due to a cold, breathe on a Bloodstone until it is warm and moist. Insert the warm stone into your nostril and pinch both nostrils with your fingers so that the warmth of the bloodstone permeates the head and thus loosens the flow. The sufferer should soon be able to breath freely again.*

Chrysoprase: *This crystal is ideal in cases when somebody is furious (enraged!!). Hildegard suggests placing this crystal on the throat of the person*

Garnet: *concerned and leaving it there until his anger leaves him and he calms down...... (Would you not love to have a try???)*

When suffering from head aches, Hildegard suggests placing this crystal on the head (how?) and leave it there until warmth is felt. This would set the healing process in motion

Topaz: *When your eyes are deteriorating put a Topaz in wine for three days. After that, before going to sleep stroke your eyes with the moist Topaz. After removing the crystal from the wine, it can be kept for up to five days. During this time you can dip your Topaz in this wine again and with it gently circle around each eye... This may be repeated as often as needed.*

Interesting as they are, these unorthodox treatments are history and I strongly advise against attempting to practise these remedies for obvious reasons!

In addition to these rather unconventional remedies, Hildegard also presents us with other methods, more practical and still used today. Nevertheless, it is pleasing to know that crystals were used for healing in the 12th century, however unusual the application by an eminent and highly respected lady as Hildegard von Bingen.

THE USE OF CRYSTALS IN TODAY'S TECHNOLOGY

Industry has long since recognised the properties and potential of crystals. Their uses for technological purposes go back further than one might expect and their commercial applications are many. As far back as I am aware, Crystals have been used in industry since the early part of the 20th century. Best known is the use of crystals in the earliest radios. I remember my own grandmother proudly telling us grandchildren, many times about the excitement of having her own Crystal Set. In this case the crystal's job clearly was to amplify the energy received by the antenna.

From the Atlantis story by Richard Gerber[6♦] we also learn that crystals were used in their 'energy stations' to transmute the sun's energy into usable power. Today, we have solar panels in the roofs of our houses which do a similar job. The method may differ, but it is, on balance, not vastly dissimilar from the way our ancestors used it!

With the advance of the computer/communication age, demand for commercial crystals has increased considerably. After all, what else is the famous silicon chip in our computers but quartz crystal? And what about the simple quartz watches, which are the norm today? Perhaps this may surprise the reader, but another very important client for crystals is the aircraft industry. They need tremendous quantities and with their sophisticated computers on board aircraft, their crystals have to be of very specific sizes and clarity. Today, these (artificial crystals) are grown to a specific size in laboratories in an accelerated fashion. Without crystals in commerce, a lot of our technologically geared world might not necessarily come to a standstill, but would definitely slow down considerably!

In the commercial world of today, the properties of crystals were recognised long before man was prepared to acknowledge their healing properties. There is still a great reluctance to accept that crystal energy could be applied to healing and this has caused many disputes. However, progress is being made! Since the second half of the past century, most people holding a crystal are able to feel something, which is a great step forward!

---

6 ♦ Vibrational Medicine, Richard Gerber. Bear & Company Publishing. Santa Fe, NM. US

CRYSTALS TODAY

Looking back at our crystal history, and how crystals were used in the past, may inspire faith in recognising their power and potential in healing. Living in the 21st century, we have the opportunity of taking this knowledge further and work with crystals in a positive way for the healing and well-being of humanity, the animal population, environment and our precious Mother Earth. I personally believe that healing with crystals is still in its infancy and that big strides will be made in this therapy in the not too distant future.

****

THE TRANSFORMATIVE POWER OF CRYSTALS

During the years that I have been teaching Crystal Therapy, I have seen more changes take place in the lives of my students than at any previous time in my 'teaching-complementary-therapies' career. While learning how to heal others with the help of crystals, I learned about the amazing capacity crystals have of affecting deep healing in students during their 'apprentice' period. There is an old saying, "To be an effective healer we first have to heal ourselves". I continually find this to be true with my students. Energies evoked during the healing process are amplified by the energy of crystals. The purer we are, the higher the healing vibrations capable of flowing through us. In order to reach this state of purity, it is necessary for remaining energy blocks be removed from our physical and/or auric bodies, be it mental or emotionally.

At this point some information may be in order to explain what is understood by 'auric' bodies. As most of you will know already, the physical body is surrounded by an electric magnetic energy field often called the aura. This field consists of many layers and the vibration of each 'layer' further away from the physical body, becomes finer and finer, or you might say 'subtler' As crystal healers we are in fact energy healers and as such deal with both the physical body, which is a very efficient energy system, as well as the subtle bodies. We, at the Vantol College work with the three layers immediately outside of the human body, i.e.;

1) the Etheric layer, usually up to 2-5 cm immediately next to the body
2) the Emotional Body, on average up to 20 cm away from the body and
3) the Mental body, about up to 40 cm away from the body

These measurements may vary quite a bit, depending on the physical and emotional condition of each person at any given time.

As one commences on a healing career, there is often a need for changes in almost all aspects of life. Difficult as this may be, it allows the student to become a clearer channel for the healing energy. Working with crystal energy brings this to the conscious mind in a subtle way. When a student is ready, the crystals assist by creating circumstances that force that person to take certain actions and make certain changes.

Since healing with crystals requires sensitivity, the sensing of energies is a very important part of the training. At the start of the course, students are often doubtful about their ability to 'feel' or 'sense' the energy of crystals. They erroneously assume that they lack 'sensitivity', and doubt their ability to do healing work with crystals. Yet, at the same time, they have a strong feeling of being 'called' to undertake this training. To the surprise of many (but not to those of us who teach it) positive awareness in sensitivity takes place quite soon. These changes usually start slowly, but as energy consciousness increases (aided by a few months of practical exercises that include working with and sensing crystals) the new students become pleasantly surprised. They CAN 'feel' and 'sense' energy!

My personal belief is that virtually everybody has this capacity for sensing energy. After all, our ancestors relied upon their senses and intuition for survival and, somewhere deep in our subconscious, these talents are still present, albeit dormant. It simply needs practice to revive them! Living in today's world with every kind of technology at our fingertips, there is little need to rely on our senses for survival.

Sensing and intuition play an important part in crystal healing. They are natural and essential tools for the genuine Crystal Healer and it is not by chance that energy awareness is amongst the first lessons in our crystal therapy courses. Various subtle energy exercises, with and without crystals, very quickly help the student to both sense and feel human and crystal energy. It is not always obvious, but the true teachers in this case are the crystals themselves, assisted by the high environmental energy created by their peers; a group of equally devoted and enthusiastic like-minded students.

The Crystal Therapist

To understand why sensitivity in a crystal healer is so important, let us look at circumstances affecting a successful crystal healing:

1. *The therapist, above all, must act with the purest intention to work for the highest good of the client.*
2. *The therapist must be aware of his or her personal energy and must be healthy and in sound mind. In any other circumstance, giving a treatment would be unwise and would not benefit the client.*
3. *The therapist must be able to sense the client's energetic requirements.*
4. *The therapist must have the skill and sensitivity to be able to choose the appropriate healing crystals for each client, i.e. achieving the right 'blend' of energies to attain the energy balance the client needs. The correct choice of crystals is paramount to the outcome of the treatment.*

It is important to be aware that each person, as an individual, has unique personal energies. This means that while one particular crystal may be perfect for one person, the same crystal for an identical condition may well be totally ineffective for the next client. Crystal therapists endeavour to treat the cause of the condition. Consider Mrs. A's migraine; her problem is caused by stress. Another client, Mrs. B, has an identical complaint, but the root of her condition is different, it could be a hormonal imbalance or inappropriate diet. This illustrates that each treatment is a 'one off' and completely different for each person. In short, it requires a sensitive approach by the therapist, followed by a unique treatment with carefully selected crystals.

Considering the above circumstances, our college requires a two year in-depth training to become an accredited crystal therapist. It also makes sense when you consider that the healer needs this time to develop his or her sensitivity and gain a thorough understanding of the human energy system. In addition to this, the healer has to acquire an extensive knowledge of the energetic and physical characteristics of healing crystals and how, when and where, to apply them. This is of paramount importance. A healer also needs to become aware of the deep effect crystals can have on the emotions of the client and how to deal with these situations as they occur.

Crystals affect not only the person receiving the treatment, but also work on the students during their training period. The crystals help clear away any remaining dross from past situations and each healer needs to come to terms with resolving this residue. It is an important preparation for the student who will soon be working as a professional crystal healer.

Becoming a crystal therapist is truly a passage of transformation!

To create awareness of changes in their lives while attending the crystal therapy course, our students are asked to keep a 'diary', or journal, throughout their two-year training. Towards the end of the course they are required to submit a résumé of their personal experiences during this period. When the student writes it, he or she often expresses surprise. To illustrate, I would like to quote a few excerpts from some students' Personal Journeys. (The students quoted were happy to give their consent.)

Excerpt AC

I have to confess that choosing a course of study about crystals did not prepare me for a spiritual awakening. I thought I would just be learning about the crystals and what they could do, but I had not taken into account that they would change me on so many different levels, nor that I would intuitively become so much more aware of other people's emotions and feelings.

Excerpt STB

"Just before the first weekend of the crystal course I was having problems with emotions about a man whom I had been in relationship with for five years. We had separated for about two years and I was still trying to release pent-up emotions about him. The first day of the crystal course we were taught a very basic quartz cleansing treatment. I felt buzzing and heat and a deep sense of relaxation.

That night I had a dream about my ex-partner; I was sitting behind a rock in a place I find safety in. He came over and I told him all that I needed to. He told me everything was fine and not to worry. We hugged and smiled at each other.

The next day all my negative feelings about him had gone, and I even felt that if I ever saw him again, I would feel comfortable to give him a hug! I have not had those negative feelings return."

Excerpt CR:

I have realised that many people are now learning and know about the power and potential of crystal healing. I think that memory veils from ancient days are being lifted as personal research and individual experience with crystals and stones is forming the foundation of true knowledge. I also feel that we are led by light forces to choose our own teachers to guide us along this path. I personally have become more and more aware of the personal energies of people around me and am thankful for the guidance of good teachers.

Excerpt LW:

"The crystal course, and my work and interest in crystals, has changed my outlook on life and living. Those days when I yearned to be different have gone. Now I realise that everyone is different – and difference does not have to be negative. Let's call 'different' and 'special' the same thing"

****

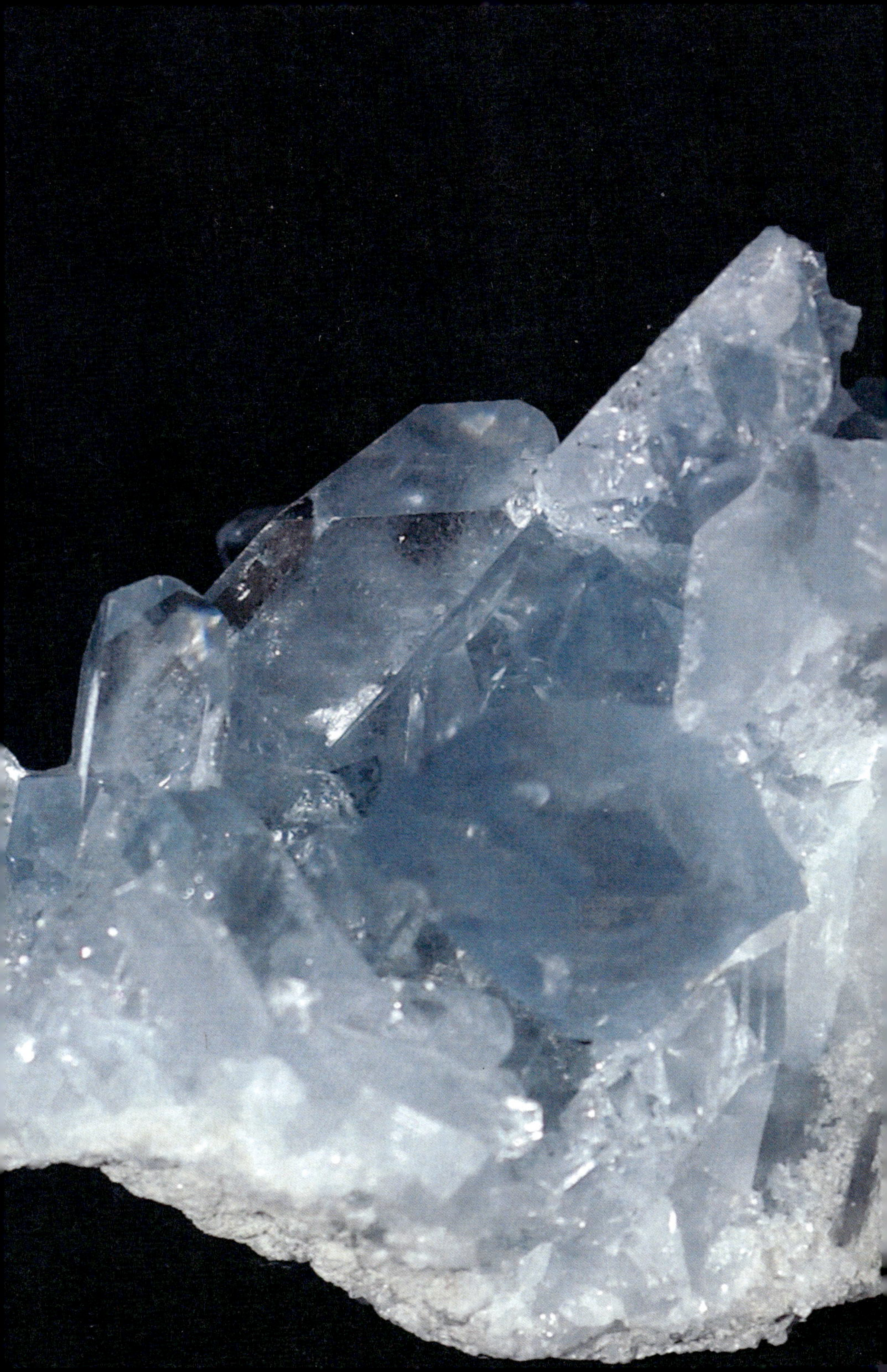

Celestite

CRYSTAL BASICS FOR PERSONAL USE

HOW DO CRYSTALS HEAL?

This is a question I have been asked many times over the years. People are intrigued by the idea that crystals **can heal** and have great difficulty believing this (until they receive a treatment from a qualified crystal therapist!). The sceptics are many and only too happy to convince anyone prepared to listen that this is yet another weird new-age therapy!

In my first answer I usually explain that crystals have energy and that crystal healing is an energy based therapy and must therefore be viewed from a totally different angle. Assuming that there are readers amongst you with a similar question such as: "How can this possibly work?", I suggest you start by looking at the human body as an energy system, although I presume that many of you reading this book are already familiar with this.

It is encouraging that Western scientists have, over the past quarter of the last century, accepted the fact, known to ancient Chinese healers for centuries, that our bodies are efficient energy systems, surrounded by an extensive energy field. In scientific circles the latter is referred to as 'electro-magnetic field', more commonly known to us, ordinary folk, as 'the aura'.

Most of us, thinking of energy, cannot help but conjure up a mind picture of an electric kettle on the boil, or pylons with heavy cables carrying electricity to places far and wide. We all rely on energy to keep our domestic appliances working efficiently and, providing that there is no hitch in the energy flow (electricity) they do the job! Now compare this to our body systems. As long as the energy continues to flow efficiently through our body, it should keep our body in good working order, i.e. the well-being of the body is usually maintained. But lo and behold if this balance is disturbed! You, as a patient, would not feel too good! Energy disturbances in our physical energy system have a detrimental affect on our health and well-being and one of the biggest offenders causing this is STRESS!

By simply living we encounter daily challenges and usually deal with them; sorting them out to the best of our ability. In most cases this is sufficient to prevent any harm being done to our energy system (our physical body). Nonetheless, when faced with an ongoing distressing situation the energy system (our body) gets overburdened. This makes it difficult for the current to continue its harmonious flow and an energy obstruction is created.

If stress situations only happen occasionally, the body can usually deal with this. On the other hand, should an upsetting condition be on-going, the energy blockages created may settle semi-permanently within a particular part of the body, and affect certain organs or systems in a damaging fashion. Eventually this may be the cause of a dis-ease. The Chinese national healing system of acupuncture is based on this principle; their acupuncturists re-balance the energy flow with the aid of gold and/or silver needles. We, as crystal healers, use crystals to achieve a similar effect.

There are many energy therapies available today which can restore the energy balance, but in my experience, as a therapist with many complementary therapies under her belt, Crystal Therapy is one of the most effective methods to restore this balance. However, I must stress here that, when using crystals to rebalance the system, crystal healing should always be carried out by a properly qualified accredited Crystal Therapist (someone who has at least completed a two year accredited course); Due to the in depth training undergone, this person understands the subtle energies of both crystals and the human energy system. She/he will be able to rebalance the natural energy flow in the physical and subtle bodies of the client and from that point onwards the body's own innate healing system will take over. We so easily tend to forget that our bodies have this efficiently built-in self-healing system. If approached from a purely technical point of view, you could look upon the crystal healer as a person who 'mends the circuit' and the body does the rest!

It is in this field where pure Quartz Crystals are leading the way! They have been used for healing since time immemorial, but we in the West are a sceptical lot and would really like some scientific proof before we go along with any belief as way out as this...!! Fair enough! But hold on; scientific recognition is just around the corner!

MICRO-CRYSTALS

It is gratifying to know that scientists have discovered, and now confirm, that we humans have an innate crystalline structure in our bodies!! They also acknowledge that Quartz crystals are capable of radiating energy and that this has a resonant effect upon the crystalline energy structure within our bodies.

To explain this further, let us take a look at Micro-Crystals. Micro-Crystals *(also referred to as 'Liquid Crystals')* are, as the word 'micro' indicates tiny, tiny crystals which are partially crystalline and partially fluid. They are probably best known for use in the flat computer and laptop screens, flat TV screens, and sun-panels, the read-out screens of our digital watches, our mobile phones and numerous industrial appliances. All these devices contain liquid micro-crystals, all be it of an artificial kind.

The interesting part is that scientists now recognise that similar Micro-Crystals also form part of our human biological make up. They discovered that these crystalline substances are mainly present in our body fluids, i.e. blood, the lymphatic fluid, and the CSF (Cranial Spinal Fluid), but also in our muscles and skeletal system. Apparently our red and white blood cells contain a lot of 'liquid crystal' and therefore display quartz-like properties.

To understand the function of liquid crystals in our body, we have to view this from an energy point of view. As explained above, the chemical substances present in the micro-crystals in our body, are also present in crystals. To understand what happens when crystals are introduced into our aura, can be explained by the Law of Resonance. To give an example; imagine you have two similar electro-magnetic objects; one has a high energy and the other is almost depleted. Place them together and the resonance between the two will cause object **A** *(high energy)* to transfer some of its energy to object **B** *(low energy)* and in doing so a balance of energy in each object has been achieved. In a similar way, balance may be restored to the body with the help of crystals because of the strong sympathetic resonance existing between the crystals *outside* and the micro-crystals inside the body.

Due to this resonance, an imbalance in the human energy system may be rectified effectively and painlessly by a qualified crystal therapist, with the help of appropriate crystals. This is where her expertise comes in; her in-depth knowledge of the human energy system, a thorough understanding of the anatomy and physiology of the human body; as well as a sound knowledge of the energetic properties and effects of a vast number of crystals. (The fact that crystals are immensely powerful tools is not always recognised by lay people and, because of this, crystals have to be used with knowledge and discretion.) [7♦]

Once our energies are re-balanced, and a healthy 'flow' is re-established; our innate healing system will once again do its utmost

---

[7] ♦ It is important to be aware that, as is the case in many other therapies, there are certain contra-indications, i.e. illnesses where crystal healing is not the best option. A qualified crystal therapist is aware of this and knows when and when not, to give a crystal healing session to her client.

to heal our body. To reiterate; the aim of crystal healing is to rebalance the client's energy flow and when this is restored, the best environment for the body to heal itself will have been re-established.

Another very important part of the treatments is that a genuine Crystal Therapist channels healing energies during the crystal therapy session, which are amplified by the crystals, thus amplifying the healing potential.

Having been the lucky recipient of a true crystal healing treatment, one is normally left with a wonderful feeling of lightness and relaxation. It is something that should be experienced to feel the true benefits. If you have never received a treatment from an experienced Crystal Therapist, why not go ahead and give yourself a treat!

To sum up, the outcome of an authentic Crystal Healing treatment creates a harmonising, and ultimately healing potential. My personal advice is that, if you have not done so already, go and give it a try! You don't have to be ill as it is also a super prescription for stress!

CHOOSING CRYSTALS

ATTRACTION TO CRYSTALS

Who can resist a beautiful crystal? Glowing, shining and beckoning you to take it into your hands and carry it home! Let us face it! We are irresistibly drawn to crystals, and there is more to it than just their beauty. Throughout history there has always been a strong connection between humans and Crystal Beings.

Crystals are living entities; they may not communicate in the way you and I do but, on an energetic level they certainly have the edge! Like us humans, every single crystal has its very own frequency. Even two look-alike Quartz crystals will have a slightly different vibration. There are crystals that help us balance our energies, others with their specific vibration may help with individual conditions, while yet others can relax us, or provide a straightforward general healing effect. Crystals are a great help when connecting to our Higher Self and the Angelic Kingdom when meditating. Besides radiating healing energies they can also support and protect us from negative energies. With so many beautiful crystals tempting us out there, the choice is vast. This might lead you to believe that it would complicate your choice, but this is not necessarily the case. There are many ways of choosing just the right crystal for you. So let us investigate!

Choosing!

Choosing crystals is one of the most enchanting pastimes, although it can be somewhat overwhelming when faced with the beautiful arrays laid out in our crystal shops! So much to choose from! Which one do I need? Which one do I want? What we really want is to choose just the Right One for us; a crystal we either want, or feel we need to help us or heal us, at this specific time. Viewing these awe-inspiring displays is pure joy! So how best go about it?

Have you ever watched children choosing crystals at a crystal exhibition, or in a crystal shop? They have no doubt at all as to which one they want. They go straight for their crystal. No hesitation! They dive into a bowl of tumble stones, pull out 'the' one with a triumphant: 'This is the one'......

The answer is simple: they have not as yet been programmed to think too hard as to which one would suit them best, reason it out like most of us do, or consider which one is the best value for money. They simply allow their intuition the freedom to choose with the result that they always go for the 'Right One'! Could we but turn the clock back!!

Choosing intuitively

If you have ever been to crystal lectures or workshops you will surely have heard the phrase: **'Crystals choose you!'** Strange as this may seem at first, it is the truth and it may help you to think of this process as a 'mutual attraction' – which it is on an energetic level!

Although hard to believe, nothing is simpler than choosing

crystals! Everybody has the innate intuition to know which crystal you need at this moment in time. All that is required is a little sensitivity. There is a part within you that knows your needs. Let us settle for 'subconscious mind'. We have all been programmed to rely on our logic and have to relearn to trust our feelings and allow our intuitive senses to come into play. Open your mind and be receptive to crystalline energy and you may surprise yourself by choosing the Right Crystal without any effort, because **your crystal will already have chosen you!**

Next time you visit a crystal shop try it out! Your attention will somehow be drawn to a certain crystal. It may not physically be the most beautiful one in the shop. But it will have a certain something which resonates with your energy! Your crystal will stand out from the crowd! Pick it up and hold it in your hands: look at its beauty. Do you like its colour? Do you sense its energy? Does it feel good in your hands? You feel you do not want to let go of it…. If it does all these things, you will invariably know that this is 'your' crystal. You may not be able to afford it at that moment, but you just cannot bear to put it back… This clearly is *the* crystal for you!

The important thing here is to simply go by your feelings. We all have this innate intuition, and just need to re-learn to trust it and all that needs is practice! Having learned it, you will be amazed how helpful this can be; not only when you are choosing crystals, but it is a great asset generally in life. Next time you visit a crystal shop, try it out!

I have had several personal experiences of crystal attractions. In one case it was a most gorgeous Quartz Crystal Sphere with a diameter of about 10". Its inclusions were breath taking with rainbows galore. It was truly beckoning me. Alas on finding out its price, I expressed my apologies to the very understanding wholesaler (who *knew* it was for me) explaining that sadly at this time there was not the slightest chance I could find the necessary cash. Arriving home I felt quite dejected and looked at my financial commitments from every which way, trying to solve this unsolvable situation … No way could I justify this purchase…

A year and a half later at the same exhibition, I was once again drawn to this particular stand and there 'he' was again! Shining and more beautiful in my eyes than before! No doubt as delighted to see me as I was about seeing him again. Would he still be able to come to me? I noticed that the price had dropped considerably. Chatting with the wholesaler (a truly spiritual person) I learned that he had shown this crystal on all the exhibitions he had attended over the past 18 months, but no one had shown the slightest interest in it. He truly felt that this crystal was meant to go to me so that I could do group work with it. With this in mind he lowered the price still further, letting me have this amazing crystal at his cost price. I still bless this exceptional wholesaler who generously helped both this crystal and me to carry out our spiritual tasks. This is clearly a case where the crystal chose me.

Meanwhile, having settled in the crystal environment of my home and classes, he is very happy doing what he set out to do, assisting in group work with both meditation and practical sessions. This is his special contribution to human transformation at this time.

Choosing Mentally

If you want to choose your crystals mentally, you need in the first place to be aware of your personal energy requirements. Secondly, you should know a fair bit about the effects and properties of crystals in order to be sure to choose the crystal with the correct energies. A crystal with energies that compliments your own at this particular stage of your life. All this will take a fair amount of time and study. However, some examples are as follows:-

Type Of Crystal	Sample	General Effects
Clear	Clear Quartz	healing and balancing effect on mind and body
Translucent/Milky	Rosequartz	healing effects our emotions
Dense	Sodalite Rhodochrosite	strengthens and has healing effect on our physical bodies
Irregular spots	Snowflake Obsidian	inspiring for stable and well-balanced people
Irregular Lines	Rutilated Quartz *	can be helpful when there is a need to break a certain pattern in one's life
Regular lines	Tourmaline	promotes harmony in one's life and peaceful energies

* The more lines or blotches there are in a crystal; the stronger the effect.

The above table contains but **very rough** guidelines. Another factor which might cause confusion is that you will often find crystals which are not 100% 'pure'. An example of this is a Quartz crystal which is part clear and part milky. This, of course, changes the energies and means that it will be somewhat different from those which are totally clear.

Choosing with the help of your pendulum

For those amongst you who are happy and confident using the pendulum, this is a very straightforward way of choosing the Right Crystal for you. You simply ask the crystal that appeals to you, if it is right for you at this time and you will receive an answer. Two things are happening at this stage. Firstly, the pendulum picks up the energies projected from the crystal, while simultaneously, your own body broadcasts its energetic 'needs' and like a good computer will respond positively to the crystal which can supply those energies you mostly need at this particular moment.

Colours

Colours have a vibration of their own. Perhaps you have experienced a colour therapy session, where colours are used to soothe, energise or enhance well-being. As you already know, each type of crystal has its own vibration, and the colour added to its innate frequency creates its individual energy. Therefore, in addition to the general table above, it might be of help to know a little of the effects of colours. An overview would be as follows:

Colour	Overview Of Effect
Pink	Unconditional love for self and others
Red	Vital energy, encourages will power and determination
Yellow/Gold	Promotes clarity of thinking - brings joy
Orange	Stabilises energy when one feels low
Brown	Steadies one's physical body - brings you 'back to earth'
Green	Generally harmonises and brings peace and healing
Turquoise	Stimulates the immune system
Blue	Calms, soothes inflamed conditions - great general healer
Violet/deep Purple	Helps to relate to one's Higher Self - aids inspiration Stimulates innate grace and wisdom
Black	Strengthens - brings one 'down to earth'

As time goes on you will find a method of choosing crystals which is comfortable to you. You may want to try all of the above and will no doubt settle for the one that best suits you.

Sensitivity training

Sensitivity is an important part of training in crystal healing courses. Not only do you get to know the properties of crystals, but the students also learn how to discriminate between;

- clean crystals and crystals in need of cleansing
- crystals which have little energy and crystals brimming with positive energy
- crystals which simply want to be decorative and
- crystals for healing purposes

Being sensitive also means that, when you do occasionally come across a crystal that has absorbed a lot of not-so-nice environmental or human energies, you become aware of it. When there is only a slight amount of negative energies the crystal in question can easily be cleansed. It happens occasionally that this is not possible and can have the effect of making you quite unwell. An example of this is as follows: One of my newer students came into the class with a certain crystal he wanted me to sense. He did not want to show it, but just wanted to see what I felt... Trusting him I allowed him to place it into my hand...

I never experienced an electric shock in my life, but this crystal literally 'floored' me. It immediately drained all energy out of me. Some curious students standing around wanting to see what was going on, caught me, while his nice looking crystal hit the floor (almost followed by me!). I felt sick and faint and all my chakras were adversely affected. My co-teachers worked on me with healing and the 'right' crystals to bring me back to a semblance of normality. It took me a good 24 hours to recover from this experience! The student whose crystal it was had picked it up from a stall and admitted 'It was not feeling too good', but as his sensitivity needed some more developing at the time, it did not have the disastrous effect on him which it produced in me! It was a great lesson in discernment for my students, but one I would rather teach about than demonstrate!

Perhaps this is a good place to stress the importance of choosing your crystal carefully because, as explained above, you may very occasionally come across crystals which carry negativity (more will be explained about this in a later chapter). Try and develop your sensitivity which will be of great benefit, not only when working with crystals, but generally in life. Learn to trust your intuition and, remember, there is always your pendulum!

****

CLEANSING CRYSTALS

It is important to remember that the initial cleanse after acquiring your new crystal, is the most important one and will in most cases need more time than successive cleansing sessions.

Having found your own special crystal, either in the crystal shop or at an exhibition, you are dying to take it home and hold this newly acquired treasure in your hands to admire it and sense its energies. If you are a therapist or into healing, you cannot wait to work with it a.s.a.p.! But hold on a moment!

At this point it is very important to be aware that crystals absorb energy as well as amplify and radiate it. Therefore, to benefit from your crystal's pure energies, you first need to clear it from any vibrations which are not of its own. In short, your crystal needs a good cleanse. This cannot be emphasized enough! Before you can heal or meditate with your crystal, it should be 100% cleansed from vibrations collected before it came to you, only then can you can work with its pure energies!

The moment a crystal is being touched by someone, or finds itself in her or his aura, the crystal will react to that person by first absorbing their energies and secondly starting to "work" on that person trying to create the balance he or she needs. Having absorbed this person's energy pattern and reacted to it, it will, when it is being held by the next person try to respond in the same way. Alas this does not work and we have one poor little confused crystal on, or more literally, 'in' our hands...

By the time your crystal has been excavated, cleansed and sorted, shipped to a wholesaler, moved to a retailer and been touched by a dozen or so would-be purchasers in the shop, your crystal is completely traumatised; unless it was lucky enough to have gone through the hands of caring people somewhere along the line to you! Either way by the time your buy it, it usually is in dire need of a good cleanse.

CLEANSING METHODS
Beware of Salt Water!

One of the most published cleansing methods is to put your crystals in salt water..... Ouch! Poor crystals!!! Yes it does cleanse, but also harms them permanently. Believe me, there are many safe and effective methods to achieve cleansing without harming your crystals!

When I was new to crystals many years ago, I read about this so-called 'ideal' method, advocated in virtually every crystal book which happened to come my way, and with the best intentions soaked my first treasures into salt water. When taking them out after this cleanse I got a shock. They felt different, yes clean, but hurt. Something was definitely amiss and this method, suggested by many, was not the one for my crystals! I wasted no time to find other safe methods, all of which worked well. At the same time I needed to find out exactly why cleansing crystals with salt harmed them. It took a little while to figure this out. Finally, with the help of a scientific friend, we discovered the physical reason, which is in fact quite simple. To start with she suggested I take a good look at salt? Yes, kitchen salt, preferably rock salt, where the crystals are larger.

Salt consists basically of a lot of tiny, tiny crystals. Like most of us you may at some time have cut your hand and accidentally got salt in it: "Ouch"! Yes it does cleanse, but at a cost! The effect is similar when we place our crystal in salt water. The solution will penetrate the tiniest fissures in this crystal and starts its abrasive cleansing process. Admittedly, your crystal will come out clean but, if you are not sensitive you may be unaware of the discomfort of your crystal. If a crystal is left in a salt water solution for 24 hours or more, or if this abrasive cleansing process is repeated several times you will notice that your once beautiful smooth crystal feels rough and pitted It has also lost its shining exterior.

Being aware of the harm salt does to crystals, I have been carrying out a crusade against **Using Salt to Cleanse Crystals** to the amusement of my students, who call it my 'fetish' and cannot stop teasing me! However, the important thing is that I get the message across! Seriously, it is a continuous struggle. Most people have by now read numerous crystal books and been brain washed that this is THE method. A great pity! Especially since there are many gentler ways of achieving clean crystals!

I am living in hope that this book converts YOU... If it only achieves that, the exercise of writing this book will have been worth while !

CLEANSING IN WATER (APPLIES TO NON POROUS CRYSTALS)

This is by far the simplest way of cleansing. Spring water is great, but rainwater, or even tap water, will do the job equally well. The duration of cleansing depends on the amount of negativity the crystals have absorbed. This crystal bath may last from 1 to 3 hours, or even days, depending on the 'state' of the crystal. If you are sensitive, you may feel or know when the crystal is cleansed. If you are familiar with pendulum use, you can check to ascertain when the cleansing process is finished.

CLEANSING WITH FLOWER ESSENCES
(APPLIES TO NON POROUS CRYSTALS)

This method is simple and faster and the ideal essence to use is

Crab Apple. Most of you reading this book are familiar with the Bach Flower essences, which are widely available (for suppliers see reference at end of book). Crab Apple is the great cleanser and does a wonderful job speedily. All you need do is put a few drops in the water used for cleansing your crystals and they will be sparkling clean in hours rather than days.

Cleansing with Incense

This method can be used on any crystal, but is ideal for soft and porous crystals, as well as for pendants and necklaces.

Use a good quality incense and hold your crystal in its curling 'smoke', gently turning the crystal around. When in need of cleansing the smoke refuses to get near the crystal. Continue to hold it there until the smoke caresses your crystal. This indicates that the crystal has been cleansed. After this stage give it a gentle rub with a soft clean cotton or silk cloth and you will be well rewarded, as your crystal will shine and be a joy to behold!

Cleansing with Light and Intention

Call upon your guides and angels for help and hold the crystal in both your hands. Call in the help of your special Guide or Healing Angel and visualise a beautiful Ray of Light coming down from up high, passing through and surrounding your crystal. This dazzling white light penetrates and purifies it from any undesirable energy it may have absorbed.

As with the incense method, this is ideal for pendants and necklaces as well as porous crystals and may in fact be used to cleanse any crystal. However, I would not advocate this for crystals in need of a really good cleanse since this would need a lot of patience as it might well take hours rather than minutes!

Cleansing by Moonlight

When the Moon is waning it is cleansing time for planet Earth, but when she is waxing she brings in new energy. Most of us rarely think of the energetic impact the moon has on the life of our planet, which is considerable. Crystals are affected as much as we are, and you can take advantage of this natural phenomenon by cleansing your crystals during the waning period. All you need do is place your crystals outside on a clear night when the moon is waning, i.e. 'getting smaller'. One night is usually sufficient, unless you have a badly affected crystal, in which case you may need to repeat the procedure.

By the way, it is not effective placing them indoors behind glass on your window sill. It will work, but takes a lot more time. This method is ideal for all known crystals.

Burying crystals

Now we come to the tricky part! Yes, this is a very effective method for heavily 'polluted' crystals, but it is also rather hazardous! Once crystals are returned to Mother Earth, they believe they have 'done their job' and returned home! Freedom! This is their opportunity to go and find a comfortable place to recover after having been badly affected! They know this is a time to heal and also know where to find the best (energy) spot, which is rarely the one you have chosen!

This is exactly what happens. You bury a crystal in your garden, carefully marking the spot with a stick or whatever you have handy but, when you intend to retrieve it three days later, you may well find it gone! Did you really have the right spot? Yes, you did! You dig around the spot. No crystal! What is likely to happen (and what happened to me) is that you may be digging at the far end of your garden a couple of years later and, WOW! There is a crystal you buried what seems ages ago!

If burying is your chosen method, I strongly advise you to invest in a large flower pot, fill it with clean earth and bury your crystal in it. This means you can safely retrieve a beautifully clear crystal in three (or more) days' time.

This method is ideal for heavily 'polluted' crystals, in which case it may well take weeks rather than days, but this is not suitable for porous crystals.

CLEANSING BY SOUND

Sound created by Tibetan or crystal bowls, Tibetan bells or tuning forks, create a very high vibration and submitting crystals to this reverberation is painless cleansing. This vibration is of a much higher note than the negativity the crystal absorbed and can therefore transform these energies.

Gently sound the bowl or bells one to three times over the crystals. This is usually sufficient to cleanse them. It is a simple and effective method, provided the crystals are not too contaminated. This is suitable for all crystals.

CLEANSING ON A CLUSTER

If you are lucky enough to have a large Quartz cluster, you can place any of the smaller crystals on it for both cleansing and energising. You can leave them there for a day or more, or until you need the crystals again.

HOW DO YOU KNOW IF YOUR CRYSTALS ARE CLEAR?

This is one area where your 'Pendulum know-how' comes into its own (if you are new to pendulum use, please revert to the appropriate chapter for 'how to'). After your crystals have been cleansed with your chosen method, check with your pendulum by asking your crystal if it is clear. If the cleansing has not yet finished, repeat the process until your crystal is completely free from negativity. As time goes by and you have been working with crystals for a time you will be able to tell by 'feeling' or even by simply looking at your crystal whether or not it is in need of a cleanse. Until that time your pendulum can be of immeasurable help.

Which crystals need cleansing?

Cleansing crystals is not necessarily restricted to crystal therapists working with crystals on a daily basis in the healing arena, but it is very important that it be practised by anybody using crystals for meditation or, simply for crystals 'decorating' the home. These crystals do a tremendous job; they may working for Peace and Harmony in the house or, in the case of Rosequartz, contribute to a loving caring atmosphere. Wherever crystals are involved in what is for them a working environment, they are in need of a good cleanse every so often.

Once you have established a rapport with your charges, you will soon be able to tell when they are in need of a bath or an incense cleanse. Do not delay if you want your crystals to continue working on your behalf. Give them their needed cleanse and finish the procedure by gently rubbing your crystal with a clean cotton or silk cloth. Your reward will be a glowing and radiating crystal.

Jewellery

One area often overlooked by the most sincere crystal lover is gems set in jewellery. Gems are top quality crystals with the highest energy and should therefore be the most effective in the healing field. Ironically, these exquisite beings have the greatest need for an energetic cleanse, but rarely if ever get one. Think of pendants and rings, often set with beautiful gems, worn by their proud owners day after day, either close to, or on the body. These hard working treasures become saturated by negative energies after their initial healing effect has worn off. Although they still look good to an outsider, they have no therapeutic effect on its wearer any longer. What a shame! The obvious answer is to give them a safe and regular cleanse!

The safest way to cleanse jewellery, be it set in gold, silver or another precious metal, is by simply holding them in a good quality incense. If your beautiful diamond ring has not been cleansed for years, it may take time and a fair amount of patience cleansing it in incense, but you will find that after this initial practice, and provided it is carried out regularly, it will only take a couple of minutes. Finally, give it a gentle rub with a silk cloth and your reward will be a beautiful sparkling diamond ring, broach or necklace, once again radiating its unique and special energy.

If you are in doubt if your jewellery is a) in need of a cleanse or b) how long to hold your ring or pendant in the incense smoke before it is clean, check with your pendulum. Should your treasure need energising, the best way is to place it for a day on a clear Quartz cluster. This need not be an enormous crystal; even one with a couple of inches diameter would do the job.

All of this may seem a bit 'fiddly' but it is well worth the trouble. Your ring will be glorious and your pendant will shine but, above all, you will enjoy the beneficial energies they radiate.

Energising Crystals

If your crystals are 'working' they will need to be cleansed after each meditation or healing treatment and they may also benefit from an energising session to be ready for their next job. This practice is simple:
- Translucent crystals, i.e. clear Quartz, would benefit from being placed in clear sunlight.
- Semi translucent crystals, such as Rosequartz, Aventurine

and Amethyst and Citrine would be happy to spend an hour in the sunlight, but **must** be covered by a clean cotton cloth, e.g. a tea towel. The reason being that these crystals have been known to fade when placed in direct sunlight.
- Dense crystals, such as Jasper, Sodalite, Rhodochrosite, Bloodstone etc. would benefit by spending a night in the open when the moon is full.
- Any small crystal benefits from spending some time on a large Quartz cluster.

Summary
•To fully benefit from the positive energies of your crystals make very sure that they are 'squeaky' clean.

•Choose a method of cleansing suited to your lifestyle

•Above all, keep your cleansing methods simple. Your crystal family may well expand in time, and the need for cleansing your augmented collection also grows, therefore the simpler, the quicker, and the better!

****

PROGRAMMING CRYSTALS

What is 'programming'

In ancient times crystals were often used (programmed) as talisman and amulets for love, protection etc. Nowadays we programme crystals to help us in the process of healing.

If we substitute the word 'programmed' for 'having learned, absorbed and assimilated life's events and lessons', it gives us a clearer insight. We give little thought to the fact that, as human beings, we came into this world subtly 'programmed'! This 'programming' goes back to the very beginning of the human race and has been passed on to us with the compliments of our ancestors. Like it or not! Their primitive beliefs and ways of life were strongly influenced by the basic needs to survive while life was incredibly tough. As civilization advanced, their lives became more sophisticated (complex!). We developed ingenious ways of improving life and today we consider ourselves 'advanced human beings', yet in our genes, we still carry an incredible inheritance from all our ancestors. We may not consciously be aware of this, but over the ages we have been truly 'programmed' and have not only taken aboard our own lessons and experiences of this life time, but deep in our cells we carry memories which affect us today. These subconscious memories did not only come from our parents and grandparents, but from all past generations. The way we behave and react to life today is partly the result of this subconscious 'programming' over millennia of human life.

When we programme, or 'tune' crystals, we intentionally put a certain programme (energy) into a crystal. This is nothing new! As far as we have been able to ascertain this goes back to antiquity. Over the ages amulets and talismans have been valued and used by emperors and common folk alike. They come in all shapes and forms and in many cases programmed crystals formed an important part of these charms. Well known people in history used talismen and plenty of stories about their effects still exist.

To illustrate the importance of talisman in the past, I would like to relate a well known story purported to be told by Pliny the Elder.[8]

In those days talismen were very highly valued and the dearer the item, the more power was ascribed to it. It was for instance considered bad form to barter when purchasing a talisman. Isminius, a well known flautist at that time, loved crystals and gems. He knew of the existence of a beautiful emerald which carried an engraving of Amymone[9] on it and his heart was set on acquiring this particular gem. Not only was emerald was his favourite gem but it was also a well-known talisman. When he learned that this special crystal was offered for sale, he quickly sent one of his men to purchase it.

When his messenger returned with the treasure, he was delighted to tell Isminius that he had done a great deal on his behalf. The asking price for this treasure was 6 golden dinarii, but after a suitable time bargaining, he managed to get the price down to four golden dinarii.

Imagine the shock to the poor man who had tried so hard to please his master when, on his triumphant return with the desirable talisman, Isminius started to rent and rave at him, shouting "Don't

---

8 Famous naturalist in the first century
9 Amymone was a princess of Argos loved by the god Poseidon

you realise, you fool, that by your bargaining you have considerably diminished the power of this precious Emerald (talisman)".

WHY PROGRAMME CRYSTALS?

From previous chapters you have already seen how crystals can assist us in bringing about changes in our lives and assist in healing on different levels. Yet, there is a way of further enlisting the assistance of our crystalline friends, and that is by consciously placing a certain energy into a crystal for the higher good of either a person or situation. This will enable the crystal to powerfully assist us in a specific task, which can be of immense help to both therapist and lay person. This energy represents an explicit amplified vibration, purposely put into it by ourselves or others.

There are many reasons why we may want to programme a crystal. Perhaps it is to enhance healing, perhaps we want to deepen our meditation or bring light or enlightenment to a situation or family member. You may also want to programme a crystal to sleep better, or help you concentrate at work. I daresay each of us can think of a dozen different ways in which we would like to call upon help from our crystal friends, but if we are wise, we stick to one at a time!

CHOOSING THE RIGHT CRYSTAL FOR YOUR PURPOSE

Perhaps you are already familiar with the energies of certain crystals and this knowledge will assist you in choosing a suitable crystal for your specific purpose. As mentioned earlier, all crystals have individual vibrations which affect our energies in different ways. This gives us many options when choosing a crystal for a particular purpose. In other words, if we want to programme a crystal for a specific purpose, we should choose a crystal which carries energies harmonious to our intention.

To give an example; you want to program a crystal to enhance self-love and self-respect, either for yourself or a friend. The crystal you would choose for this purpose should have the innate vibration compatible with this intention. In this case Rosequartz would be the obvious choice and you would certainly never consider using a crystal like Hematite or, say Jasper, for the simple reason that their vibrations are not in keeping with your purpose.

In the case of someone suffering from insomnia, you might like to consider an Amethyst since this crystal has harmonious and relaxing energies. Therefore programming a crystal to enjoy a healthy and relaxing sleep would definitely be in keeping with Amethyst's inherent energies. Obviously, a stimulating crystal like Bloodstone would be contra-indicated for this purpose!

It pays to take care choosing the right crystal for the right purpose as this makes all the difference to the ultimate effect. To summarise; the crystal you decide to use for your specific purpose should be in keeping with its natural energies.

Is your Crystal happy to accept his 'allocated' job?

Another important point to remember is to ask your chosen crystal if it would be happy to be dedicated for x...... purpose. This can be done in meditation, but if you have difficulty getting an answer, use your pendulum. You can do this by holding your pendulum over the crystal in question and simply ask: "Are you happy to be dedicated to healing?" (or whatever intention you have in mind). As you do this you may discover that crystals have their own agenda which often differs from the purpose you have in mind. You might think that a certain person would be excellent to do a certain job for you, yet this might not be what that particular person would like to do. Crystals are in this way not unlike people; programming them against their 'will' is not only counter-productive, but lacks respect for the individual crystal. Each crystal has its own 'personality' just like each human and we should honour their purpose.

CLEANSING

To ensure that your chosen crystal will be able to absorb the new programme, it is essential that this crystal be thoroughly cleansed before the dedication. I suggest you take a look at the methods described in the Cleansing chapter and choose the one suitable for the type of crystal you are going to programme.

PROCEDURE OF PROGRAMMING

One of the most effective ways to programme crystals, with a view to enhance their energy for a specific purpose, is to dedicate (or programme) them. There are many ways to achieve this, but the one used in our college is simple and effective and is set out further on in this chapter.

You may remember from an earlier passage in this book that the moment you hold a crystal in your hands, its energy connects and reacts to your personal energies. The crystal will first absorb your energies and subsequently 'broadcast' the synergistic energies (the crystal's and yours) which have been created. Let us assume that you have a crystal which you want to programme to help you in a difficult situation. This means that every time you hold this programmed crystal, or bring it into your aura, it sends out this specific healing synergy created to assist either you or a certain situation. This will result in an energetic change which takes place in your personal system, creating the desired energy which will assist in bringing about the conditions for which it has been tuned, be it for personal harmony, or healing.

THE DEDICATION

Having decided on the purpose and work you intend to do with your chosen crystal, it is now time to prepare yourself. Programming, also known as 'tuning', is a very individual act of dedication, both for yourself and your crystal. Think of it as a sacred ceremony, because in doing so you create the right atmosphere which, coupled with intend, will affect the final outcome. You may well have your own favourite method of programming, and that is great, but in order to get you started you might like to use the method set out below, which is the one used in the Vantol College.

It is worth taking trouble to choose the right place to carry out your dedication. If you are lucky enough to have a sanctuary or healing room, that would be ideal. If not, choose a place in your house which is calm and peaceful and where you will not be disturbed for 20 minutes or so.

A peaceful frame of mind creates the right atmosphere. To help achieve this, light a candle and incense stick and relax. You could sit in your favourite chair or cross- legged on the floor. The main thing is to sit how and where you are most comfortable. Take a couple of deep breaths, breathing in light, exhaling tension, and go into a meditative state, all the while holding your chosen and cleansed crystal. When you feel ready, hold the crystal in both hands at the height of your heart chakra and say the following out loud:

"I purify this Crystal in the Light and Love
Of our Father Mother God[10]*"*
"May those Energies, which do not belong to this crystal,
be transformed into Light"
"And may only the true energies, which are inherent in
this Crystal
Remain and be amplified"
"I dedicate this Crystal to…….(e.g. healing)"

Having said this dedication, visualise the condition you wish to attain with the help of this crystal, in your mind. Programming means projecting the desired thought form (energy) into your crystal and it is therefore very important that you visualise this strongly

---

10   You can instead insert the name of the Highest Being according to your personal belief.

and transfer this energy into your crystal.

Let us assume you intend programming an Amethyst for a healthy sleeping pattern; to achieve this visualise yourself soundly and peacefully asleep. Next 'see' yourself waking up in the morning, feeling full of energy and well-being. (Whatever pattern you choose, your visualisation should be very positive and as strong as you can make it.)

Holding this vision in your mind, gentle blow on to your crystal three times. With each breath you visualise projecting this vision (thought form) into your crystal, which is precisely what is happening. Your breath carries the vibration of your mind picture and the crystal receives and stores it and will subsequently 'broadcast' it.

Having completed the ceremony, thank your crystal for making itself available for you and take great care of it. From now on, whenever you are holding this crystal, it will send these vibrations out and assists you by bringing the desired energy pattern into manifestation.

You have now acquired a very special crystal. Its energies are unique and it will work in a much focussed way. Once you have programmed it and when you are not working with it, keep it in a special place and let nobody else touch it. Remember that the moment this crystal is touched by anyone but you, it will try to work with that person. What in fact happens is that since everybody's energies are different, neither this person, nor you, after somebody else has held it, will benefit. The poor crystal will be confused since it was programmed to work with your energies and yours only. After being touched by someone else, its energies have changed and the best you can do in this case, is to cleanse it completely and start all over again!.

PROGRAMMING FOR OTHERS

You can also programme a crystal for a friend, a relative or somebody else who needs help. This is very powerful because you do this out of concern for the other person, i.e. with love, and the outcome will be a very special and effective crystal.

When programming for another person you follow the same procedure, but slightly change the text in the last line. For instance if you want this crystal dedicated to healing for this particular person you would phrase it as follows:

"I dedicate this Crystal to the healing of (name)..................."

After this ceremony carefully wrap this crystal in a piece of clean cotton, silk, or new tissue paper and give it to the intended person with your love. Tell her or him that this crystal is exclusively for them and that she/he should not let anybody else touch it. Although you have touched it and dedicated it on their behalf, your purpose was "love". This means that a very special energy was added, i.e. the Love Energy, which carries the highest vibration and therefore makes it even more special and unique.

If you have never programmed a crystal, do have a go at it. You will sense how much stronger its energy is after your dedication and the crystal in question will be visibly glowing! Crystals love working for and with us, as much as we love working with them. So don't let us disappoint them!

****

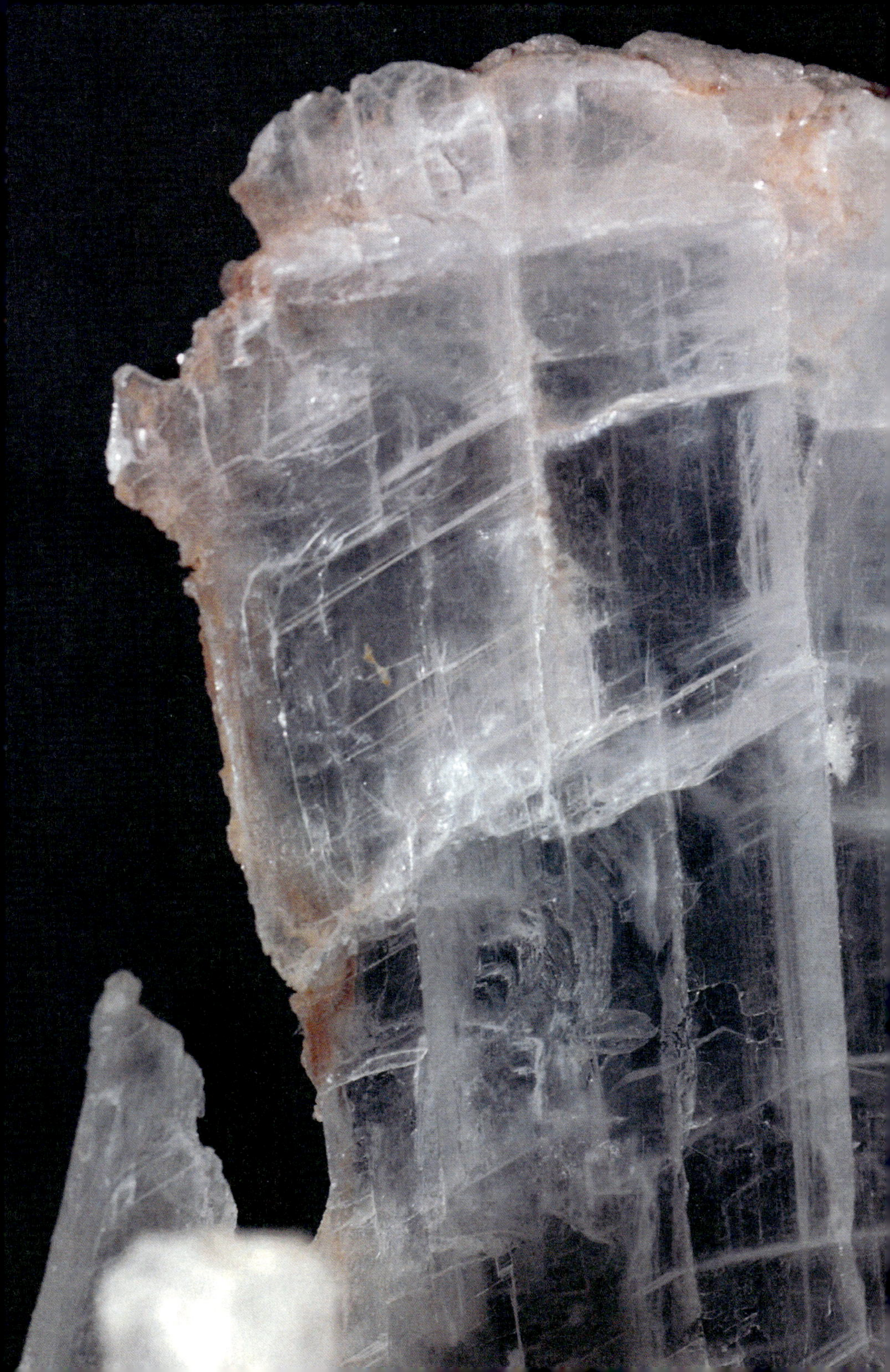

Selenite

CRYSTALS AS A MYTH

THE MYSTICAL PENDULUM

There is always a curious and immediate interest whenever anyone is using a pendulum. It has an air of mystery! People are in awe of the 'mysterious forces' which cause the pendulum to swing. Yet, there is a very straight-forward explanation as to how and why the pendulum works.

When you want an answer to a certain question but do not trust your own judgement; you would appreciate a second opinion, but a) there is nobody around for you to ask and b) it may be a question you would rather not want to share. At this point you remember your Pendulum! Surely 'it' will give you the perfect answer…. Well, sorry to disappoint you! The idea is great, but in practice it does not necessarily work quite that way. (If it did many a clairvoyant would be out of a job…..!)

Yes, your pendulum will give you an answer but, if you desperately wish something, or have in mind what you would like the answer to be, it will most certainly comply! Is that an unbiased answer? You might just as well not have bothered and act on what you wanted anyway. So let us try and unravel this phenomenon and gain an insight on how the pendulum truly works. The explanation below may throw light on this 'mystery'.

How does a pendulum function?

Have you ever wondered where the answers come from? Frequently we do not realise that the perfect answer is already within us. When you ask a question and use a pendulum, it simply amplifies the answer you subconsciously know is right. To give an example: you are purchasing a crystal and want to know if this is the right one for you. All you need do is either tune into the crystal and get a feeling or sensation that this one is right for you or, if in doubt, hold the pendulum above it, and ask "Are you the right crystal for me at this time?" The crystal's energy will connect with your personal energy and thus 'suss out' if its energy will complement or help your energies. Your subconscious mind knows the reply and the pendulum will amplify this by moving it in the appropriate direction giving you a 'yes' or 'no' answer. In this way the pendulum brings the answer into your conscious awareness.

There is nothing mysterious about the workings of a pendulum and there is no specific secret. The scientific answer would be the production of a 'synergistic mix' of personal energies with those of a particular crystal. If it is compatible with your energies the answer will be yes, if not, it will also inform you accordingly!

With a little practice anyone can learn to use a pendulum. A few people may experience some difficulty to start with, but with a little perseverance you will soon be well away! I have found again and again with new students that they are pleasantly surprised when, trying to use a pendulum for the first time, it really responds! In their excitement of discovering this new art, they are often carried away and will ask all sorts of frivolous questions, and be disappointed when it results in equally frivolous answers! (The favourite one being "Will I meet my favourite partner soon?") The pendulum is not a toy, but simply an aid to bringing into conscious awareness information that we know deep down.

WHICH TYPE OF PENDULUM IS BEST FOR ME?

On the one hand you may be lucky enough to enjoy the ultimate luxury of a gold or silver pendulum, but equally effective results can be obtained by something as simple as a button on a piece of string! Your choice is very personal, but it is most important that you work with a pendulum that feels comfortable in **your** hands. The choice is vast. Pendulums are available in all shapes, sizes, weights and materials. Some are made of wood, others may be glass, china, copper, silver and of course there are crystal pendulums. There are simple ones such as a small piece of natural rough Quartz crystal; equally you can find stunningly beautiful faceted crystal pendulums. Several of my students use a tumble stone on a piece of silk or cotton and it works 'a treat'! Although shape does not matter, pendulums which taper down at the bottom are very comfortable to work with . Like all else, your choice is very personal and depends on everyone's individual taste (and of course finances!)

Weight too, is important. Some people like their pendulum to be quite weighty, while others prefer a pendulum which is not too heavy. The length and size of the chain too are a personal choice. Some people like a short string, others prefer a long or medium one. If you intend to work with a pendulum it is worth taking a little trouble choosing the right one for you as a pendulum becomes a good friend in time. Whichever you decide on, make sure it feels good in your hands, so that you can use it with pleasure and confidence.

ESTABLISHING YOUR PERSONAL YES AND NO

Before you start working with your pendulum it is essential to find your personal 'Pendulum Pattern'. This means you should know how the pendulum moves to give you the correct answer, i.e. which direction indicates '**YES**' for you and also find out in which direction it swings to tell you '**NO**'. The direction in which pendulums move to give these answers differ from person to person. For many people '**YES**' is indicated by a clockwise swing and '**NO**' by an anti- clockwise movement. Yet for others 'yes' may mean that the pendulum moves vertically and for 'no' it moves horizontally. In order that you may work efficiently with your pendulum, it is essential to first establish your 'Personal Pendulum Directions'.

STARTING TO USE YOUR PENDULUM

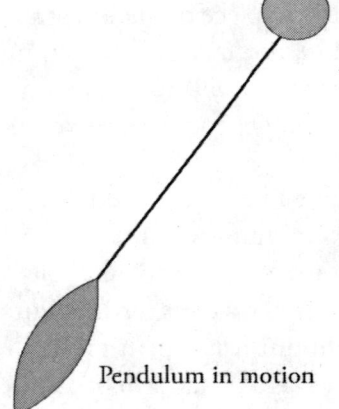

Begin by settling yourself comfortably in a chair, preferably at a table, so that your own chakra energies do not interfere. (At a later stage when you are a 'practised' dowser, you will be able to disregard these energy distractions!). Be as calm and relaxed as you can - both in mind and body.

Place your right elbow on the table to steady it, while holding the pendulum between thumb and index finger in your right hand in front of you (if you are left handed you may prefer to hold it in this hand) and ask: '**What is YES for me?**' staying as relaxed as possibly, and try not to think of anything specific. Watch your pendulum and expect an answer. If this is the first time you use it, it may well take a little while before the pendulum moves. Do not despair. You will find that it will eventually start to move. Whereas for most of us it will move slowly to begin with, for a few people it will swing fast quite soon, although this is the exception! Whichever direction it moves will be your answer. This particular movement will establish your personal '**YES**'.

The next step is to find out what '**NO**' is for you. Repeat the above procedure, but change the question to: '**What is NO for**

me?' Remember that relaxation is very important when you first start your dowsing career, so once again clear body and mind from external thoughts and concentrate on nothing but the question. Hold this question in your mind until the pendulum once again begins to move. This direction indicates '**NO**' for you.

Should you experience a difficulty in getting the pendulum to move, it may be helpful to get assistance from somebody who is a good dowser. With their expertise and energy they can often assist you to establish your personal **YES** and **NO** and help you on the way.

Once you have discovered your personal **yes** and **no** movement, practise as much as you can. Dowsing is inherent in all of us, but if you have not applied it in this lifetime, it has been dormant so far. It is a skill, and like all skills you need training. Make a regular time and spend 5 minutes a day practising and you will soon acquire the art of dowsing.

ANSWERS TO YOUR QUESTIONS!

It is important to remember that your intent, when using the pendulum, has a strong bearing on the answer. Hence we should always try to keep completely neutral when asking a question (which can be difficult when you desperately want the answer to be "yes"!).

To give an example: Imagine you see a gorgeous looking crystal which you would love to take home, but it has not chosen you... You really covet it and with the help of your favourite pendulum ask: "Would you like to come home with me?". (At this point it is really difficult to be impartial – if not impossible!) However bear in mind that the crystal in question may have another agenda – and it is not working with you! If you succeeded in being impartial, the answer in this case may well be a disappointing **NO**.... You try it a second and perhaps a third time, hoping the first answer was wrong, and if you really want it – and did not manage to be neutral, the pendulum will undoubtedly say **YES** the third time, because you desperately want it! Your desire superseded the true answer. The lesson being that you have to be scrupulously honest and unbiased. Like all lessons, this takes practice!

Phrasing your question

It is important that the question we ask is short and to the point. Remember you are asking your subconscious mind to give you the answer. Long and complicated questions will only confuse the issue and make it difficult to get a true answer. To recap:

- Your question should be simple, straightforward language.
- Keep the sentence SHORT. The simpler and shorter, the better
- Keep your mind clear and free from external thoughts and concentrate on the question.

Keeping to theses simple 'rules' will help to receive true answers.

Practising your new skills

If you are a newcomer to the art of dowsing, I suggest you begin with an object which carries a strong energy, such as a quartz crystal. This will create a faster reaction from your pendulum and give you the confidence that you CAN do it. With practice you will build up your dowsing skill sensitivity in no time and will also be able to practise on objects with lesser energy.

Having chosen your crystal for this practise session, I suggest you follow a similar procedure in the way you asked the YES and NO questions, i.e.

- Place the chosen crystal before you on a table.
- Hold the pendulum in your right hand (left if you are left handed) , between finger and thumb, a few inches above

the chosen object.
- Ask a straightforward, question, i.e.: "Is this crystal good for me?"
- Silently keep repeating this question in your mind while you are dowsing until you receive an answer. It is important that you keep focussing on your question all the time because the pendulum is extremely sensitive to your thought vibrations and 'other thoughts' will influence the outcome, which therefore, might not be correct.
- Your pendulum will react - if not right away, do not give up. Keep on practising and it will eventually respond.

Practical Uses

There are many practical ways in which a pendulum can be of assistance to you. As a crystal healer and teacher, choosing crystals is the first thing that comes to mind. This applies to purchasing crystals or choosing crystals which can help you at certain periods in your life. Perhaps you may want to choose a crystal pendant or necklace for a friend, in which case you ask it on her or his behalf. When cleansing a crystal you could ask which method it prefers.

With the help of your pendulum allow a newly acquired crystal to show you the place in your home where it wants to 'live'. (Crystals are very choosy!). Your pendulum can also be very helpful in finding out which kinds of food are good for you, or which foods do not contribute to your health (just think of how many people are allergic to nuts, wheat, diary and other nutrients). Choosing the vitamins your body needs with the help of your pendulum is another useful practice. As you become a practised dowser, you will find there are many, many ways where your little instrument can help and it is definitely worth while getting to grips with your very own 'Mystical Pendulum'

Overview
- Get to know your **YES** and **NO**
- Remain relaxed when practising
- Phrase your question short and concise
- Practise 5 minutes daily and you will soon master the Pendulum art.

You are now well on the way to become a practising Dowser!

****

CRYSTALS & RELIGION

Crystals and religion go back a long way; religion being the result of a deep-seated yearning in the human soul. As far as we have been able to trace history, people have been searching for an answer as to 'why' and 'wherefore' are we on this earth, living a life which, on the surface of it, leaves a lot to be desired for the greater part of humanity. Yet, there have always been enlightened people, seers and sensitives, who were like beacons of light and were fortunate because they knew the answers. They were the leaders of their clan, their tribe, their often extended family, etc. Aware of energy and an existence beyond this earthly life they used their knowledge and power to assist people in the trials and tribulations of life's challenges.

These enlightened leaders were the shamans, priests, rabbi or elders, each under a cloak of a different religion. They made maximum use of their intimate knowledge of energy and crystals, enabling them to channel information from High Sources. With their knowledge of energy they built chapels, churches and places of worship on leyline crossings in early mediaeval days. Leylines are part of the earth's energy system and carry energy through the earth in a similar way the meridians do this for the human body.

At these leyline crossings you will find a tremendous amount of energy. These early church priests and elders were aware of this and would tap into this energy. At best it made it possible for them to give inspired sermons and healing, but in many instances they would use it for personal gain. To this day you will find altars of many ancient churches on crossings of leylines. If you want to check this, take your pendulum with you on a nice sunny day and visit an old church in your vicinity. You will, in nearly every case, find a Leyline crossing on the altar.

At the time of building these places of worship, these leylines carried positive energies. Alas, churches were in many cases not always used for the greater good (a gross understatement!) and due to the misappropriation of energies, a legacy of negative energy was left, affecting the purity of the leylines and consequently the energy of a once sacred place. If you are sensitive to energies you may find it quite hard to stay in these places for any length of time.

I have had many personal experiences of this. The first takes me back longer than I care to remember. At the time I was living in a relatively small village in Holland where I attended a 'good' Catholic school where children were expected to be present at the twice weekly school mass. Every child between the ages of 8 – 12 **had** to be there (attendance notes kept!). My strict Catholic parents were all for this and I was duly packed off bright and early on school-mass-days. Unfortunately 15 minutes or so in the service, I would start to feel dizzy and subsequently fainted. Willing hands had to carry this awkward child out into the fresh air and it usually took the greater part of the day to recover from this all too frequent experience! As this pattern kept repeating itself, the local doctor was called in, only to confirm that "There is nothing wrong with this child. She is perfectly healthy and clearly puts it on" - My father, known as a pillar amongst the local Catholic community, had to be seen to be a good Catholic. As a result I was duly reprimanded and sent off to experience the ordeal again and again. Finally the headmaster had a chat with both parents and it was finally agreed that the disturbance of having to drag this lifeless child out of church was too disturbing … At long last I was excused from this twice weekly ordeal.

Many years later when I was energy aware, I passed this church and remembered those upsetting Tuesdays and Thursdays. Curiously I went in and was literally hit by a strong negative energy. I could feel the old fainting fear come over me and could not get out fast enough. On doing some research I discovered that a) the alter was built on a crossing of leylines and b) some unpleasant happenings had taken place there quite long ago. I realised now that, as an ultra sensitive child, I picked up on these energies and that my physical and subtle bodies just could not tolerate it. I have since felt similar effects in some other churches, but with acquired energy awareness it is possible to protect oneself and, of course, take the easiest option, which is a quick exit!

Back to the narrative about our ancient church leaders! The story goes that, to make the most of the energy supplied by the leyline crossings, gems were often inlaid in church altars to further increase the available energy. In some cases, the size of these gems was quite amazing and some are said to have been from 1 inch to 2 inches in diameter. These gems were the 'real thing' such as Diamonds, Sapphires, Emeralds, Rubies and Topaz. Normally, when gems are mentioned we immediately visualise these beautiful, rare and expensive members of the crystal family. In reality this was only the case in cathedrals and rich churches where they could afford these fabulous luxuries. Less well off churches would substitute these expensive gems with more affordable crystals. With a few exceptions the populace were unaware of this. In cases where, for certain ceremonies, more than usual energy was required, additional crystals might be displayed on the altar itself.

An interesting point is that the choice of gems/crystals which used to decorate the altars was roughly in keeping with the chakra colours.

Chakra	Gems used	Crystals substituted
Crown Chakra	Diamond	Clear Quartz
Brow Chakra	Sapphire	Blue Chalcedony
Throat Chakra	Emerald	Green Aventurine
Heart Chakra	Amethyst	Amethyst
Solar Plexus	Topaz	Citrine
Sacral Chakra	Ruby	Garnet
Base Chakra	Red Jasper	Red Jasper

Gems, being the superior kind of crystal, were mainly available to royalty and nobility, as well as to anyone in a high position or very rich. They were costly and therefore difficult to obtain for ordinary folk. The knowledge that crystals enlightened the mind and facilitated access to other realms, was a good enough reason not to allow anyone but rulers and religious leaders the privilege of ownership, or access to these treasures. These people enjoyed the power they wielded and under no circumstances would they allow the common folk access to these treasures. It was in their personal interest that the powerful energy radiated by crystals remains secret knowledge...

Thus crystals made their entrance into religious life thousands of years ago and played an important role. Further evidence of their powerful energies are early places of pilgrimage. At the shrine of Aphrodite in Papos, Cyprus, the Goddess was worshipped in the form of a conical black stone, probably a meteorite. At the holiest of Muslim shrines in Mecca lies another black stone, also assumed to be of meteoric origin and thousands of pilgrims pay their annual tribute to this Holy Stone.

Crystals have been used by native peoples all over the world and in most cases with integrity and reverence in their rituals. Specific crystals were worn as sacred amulets or carried in little pouches, to either help the wearer deal with a particular problem or condition, or perhaps ward off evil spirits. Certain ceremonies were used to enhance the properties of crystals to make them even more powerful. Presumably in a similar fashion we programme our crystals today. Generally, crystals were valued and respected amongst the genuine indigenous people and this is very much the case today.

There are many stories and legends confirming the use of crystals in biblical times: the prime example of this is the breastplate of the High Priest mentioned earlier in this book. It is rumoured that, in the 13th and 14th century, many manuscripts were in circulation about crystals, but that the Roman Catholic Church condemned the information in these documents and destroyed most of them. Here again, it would seem that the Church's hierarchy was none too happy that the population at large should have access to information about crystal power and were keen to safeguard this knowledge. It was clearly meant for the privileged few.

It is interesting though that, for as far as human memory stretches, the ceremony of initiating Bishops in the Roman Catholic Church, includes the Pope placing an ecclesiastical ring, inlaid with a large Amethyst Crystal, on one of the new Bishop's fingers! As every crystal lover knows, Amethyst is known as a 'spiritual' crystal. It therefore makes perfect sense that this choice of crystal is a suitable confirmation of the Bishop's high office. Similarly, when a new Cardinal is created in the Roman Catholic Church, he also, during the ceremony, receives a ring from the Pope, but this one is adorned with a Sapphire. This again appears very appropriate. Ancient Greeks credited this gem with wisdom and truth, while the Egyptian hierarchy attributed high spiritual energy to Sapphire, which protects and heals.

The foregoing illustrates that there is, and has been, a strong acknowledgment by religious leaders of different faiths of the value (power) of crystals. In most cases crystals were initially used with sincere intentions, but not necessarily always applied for the greater good! Yet, for those of us who might have any vestiges of doubt about crystals and their potential, it certainly confirms the awareness of power attributed to crystals by the leaders of the various religions and those in positions of power in the past.

****

CRYSTALS & ASTROLOGY

Whenever a prospective student is asked whether she or he already owns any crystals; the invariably proud reply is 'Oh yes! I have my birthstone and always wear it.' This is said while digging deep into a pocket and producing their treasure (often in need of an energetic cleanse).

The general belief - quite convenient for a healthy sales turnover - is that there is one appropriate crystal for each astrological sign: 'The Birthstone'. Hurray for simplicity! Acceptance of this belief certainly makes for an easy choice. Alas, the truth is different and may come as a shock to those people convinced they have been wearing their very own Personal Birthstone for years. They were convinced that this was, and still is, the one and most important crystal for them – and in a way it was. The psychology of this belief, and the 'knowledge' that this specific crystal smoothed their path, undoubtedly contributed to the expectations of the wearer.

Each crystal radiates a unique energy as mentioned earlier. You do not need to be an Einstein to work out that not everybody born under, say the sign of Taurus, is in desperate need of Emerald energy. Emerald is often labelled 'the official' Taurean crystal. By the same token, all Libras in the world do not require a Garnet to gain the benefit from its energies. Would life be that simple. If this were the case, you could divide the world's population into twelve groups, each with similar energetic needs. Each group would therefore have to have identical characteristics and needs. Perish the thought. For one thing, this would make many an astrologer redundant and there would only need to be One Official Chart, no doubt prominently displayed in jewellers' and crystal shops, showing pictures and information on the Twelve Official Birthstone Crystals.

The truth, however, appears to be somewhat different. To find out the origin of the Birth-Date-Stone-Saga we need to go way, way back, to a time when pre-Christian priests were important, revered, and part of the community in which they lived. These priests were both psychic and spiritual, and one of their duties was to attend the birth of a baby. The reason was twofold; first of all, his healing energy would assist the mother during labour and, secondly, on the baby's arrival the priest would be able to tune into the soul of this new arrival and thus know which major lessons this child had to learn during this particular incarnation.

The priest would also be aware of the child's major colour ray. Each colour ray carries a specific energy and specific crystals are purported to be carriers of these rays. Being clairvoyant, the priest would be able to inform the parents of the particular crystal which carried this ray. Equipped with this knowledge, the parents had the opportunity to provide their child with the appropriate crystal. Wearing this particular crystal, or even having it in the child's immediate environment, it filled its aura and provided the energy needed. Thus armed, it helped and supported this human being during his or her life's journey and helped him/her to deal with the specific challenges to be met in this incarnation.

As time passed, less and less priests with the necessary qualities and willingness to carry out this duty were available. No longer did they attend the births of babies. Over time, this rather lovely ritual got watered down and was eventually substituted by 'The Birthstone Chart' we are familiar with today. At best it is a placebo, which still carries energy, although not necessarily the one most needed by the individual.

I believe, that we do enter this life with certain lessons to be learned and challenges to face in order to grow spiritually. We may have to deal with a definite karma pattern which we intend to work through in this lifetime, or, at least try to! And, I am in agreement with the beliefs of the priests of old, that there are crystals which are special for each individual and are designated as carriers of one of the rays. When this crystal is carried by the person needing its special vibration, it surrounds the human with its colourful specific vibration and will support the human being in his or her individual quest of lesson-to-be-learned.

Since no official list seems to have survived, there is, as you might expect, more than one version stating which crystals are the true colour bearing ones.

This is mine:

Colour Ray	Colour Ray Bearing Crystal
Purple	Amethyst
Indigo	Sodalite
Blue	Sapphire
Pale Turquoise	Prehnite
Green	Emerald
Yellow	Citrine
Orange	Orange Calcite
Red	Ruby
Pink	Rosequartz

By now you are very likely curious to know which is **your** major colour ray and how to find it. Don't dispair. You may be surprised how easy this is and you need not be clairvoyant to 'see' this. Start by thinking of your favourite colour and you are well underway. Very likely this will reflect in the colour of the clothes you wear since you subconsciously 'know' that this is the colour/energy you need. You are drawn to wearing a specific colour because it 'feels' comfortable! Look at your wardrobe. Did you realise that there are many items of clothing, for instance, in a blue colour? If this is the case, blue is very likely your main colour ray, and therefore Sapphire might well be your Birthstone, regardless whether you are an Aries or a Leo, or any other sign.

If you have like-minded friends, you might like to get together to find out each others major colour rays. You can discover this easily by doing a little exercise as set out below:

Seat yourselves opposite one another. You may feel comfortable sitting cross-legged on the ground, or in an upright chair. It makes no difference, the important thing is to be comfortable and to be able to relax. The next thing is to decide which one of you will be the active, and which one the passive partner. It is the active partner who is going to suss out her/his friend's major colour ray.

Relax your bodies completely without crossing hands or feet. The passive friend tries not to let her/his thoughts wander, but concentrates on 'being' and enjoying peace and a sense of feeling good. The active person relaxes equally, but lightly focuses on her/his partner's aura and tunes in to it. Suddenly she/he may become aware of a colour. This may be sensed or 'seen' in one's mind's eye, in a similar way you see colours in meditation. When this happens accept the first colour that is seen or comes to mind. Don't start doubting. When the colour is mentioned to the partner, watch the reaction. Nine times out of ten, the other person can accept this. Having done this successfully, switch active and passive roles so you both can discover your major colour ray. You will both be astonished that you were able to tune in <u>and</u> got it right!

After this little exercise treat yourselves to a visit to the nearest crystal shop where you both can choose your own appropriate 'Birth stone'. You will be pleasantly surprised how good this newly chosen crystal-friend feels in your hands. Perhaps you may be lucky enough to find a pendant with YOUR crystal. When this is the case, do not linger, but buy it, and take it home and wear it - only of course after proper cleansing. One of my students told me she now does not feel properly dressed without wearing her special crystal.

****

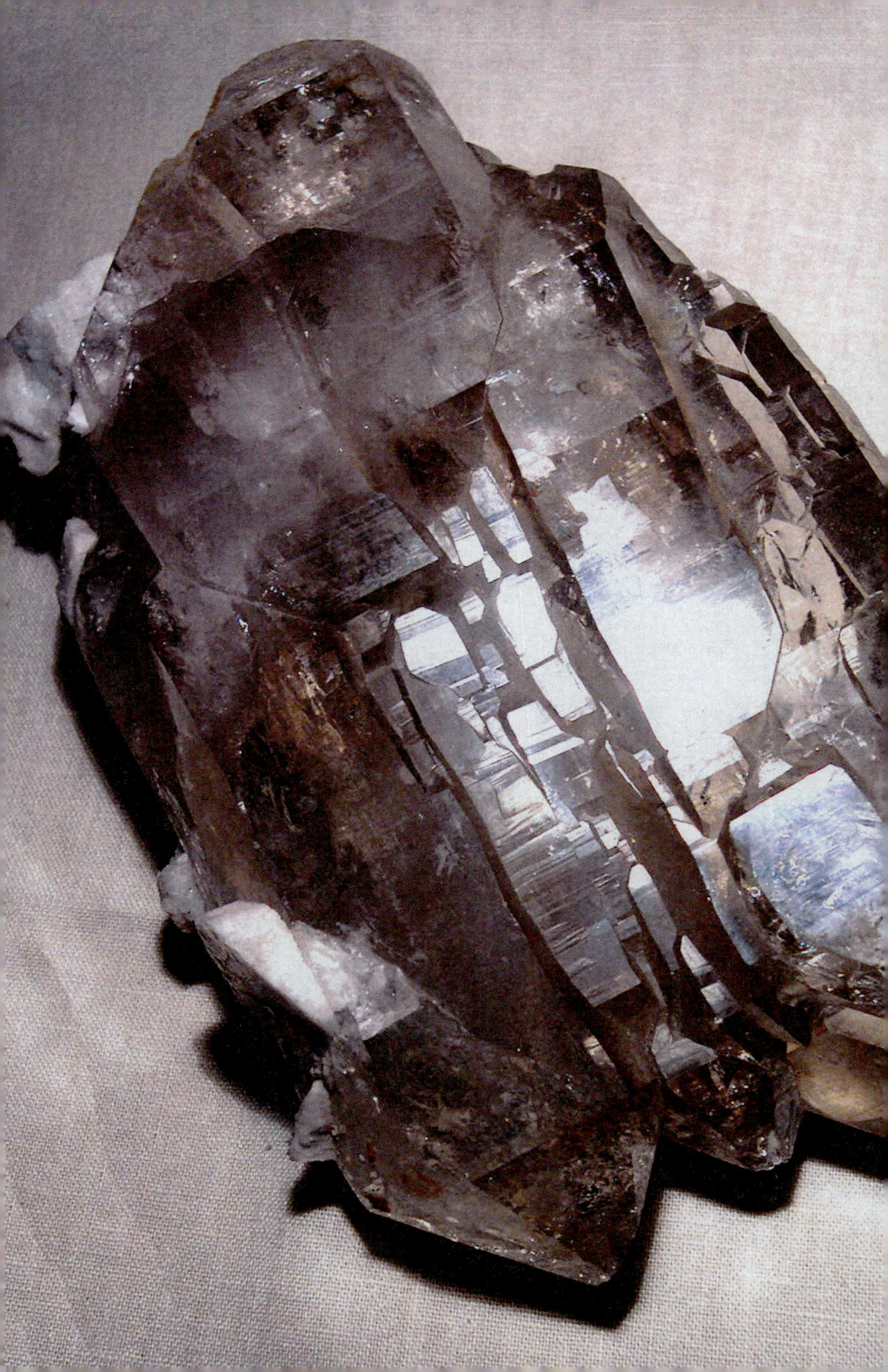

DOUBLE TERMINATED SMOKEY QUARTZ

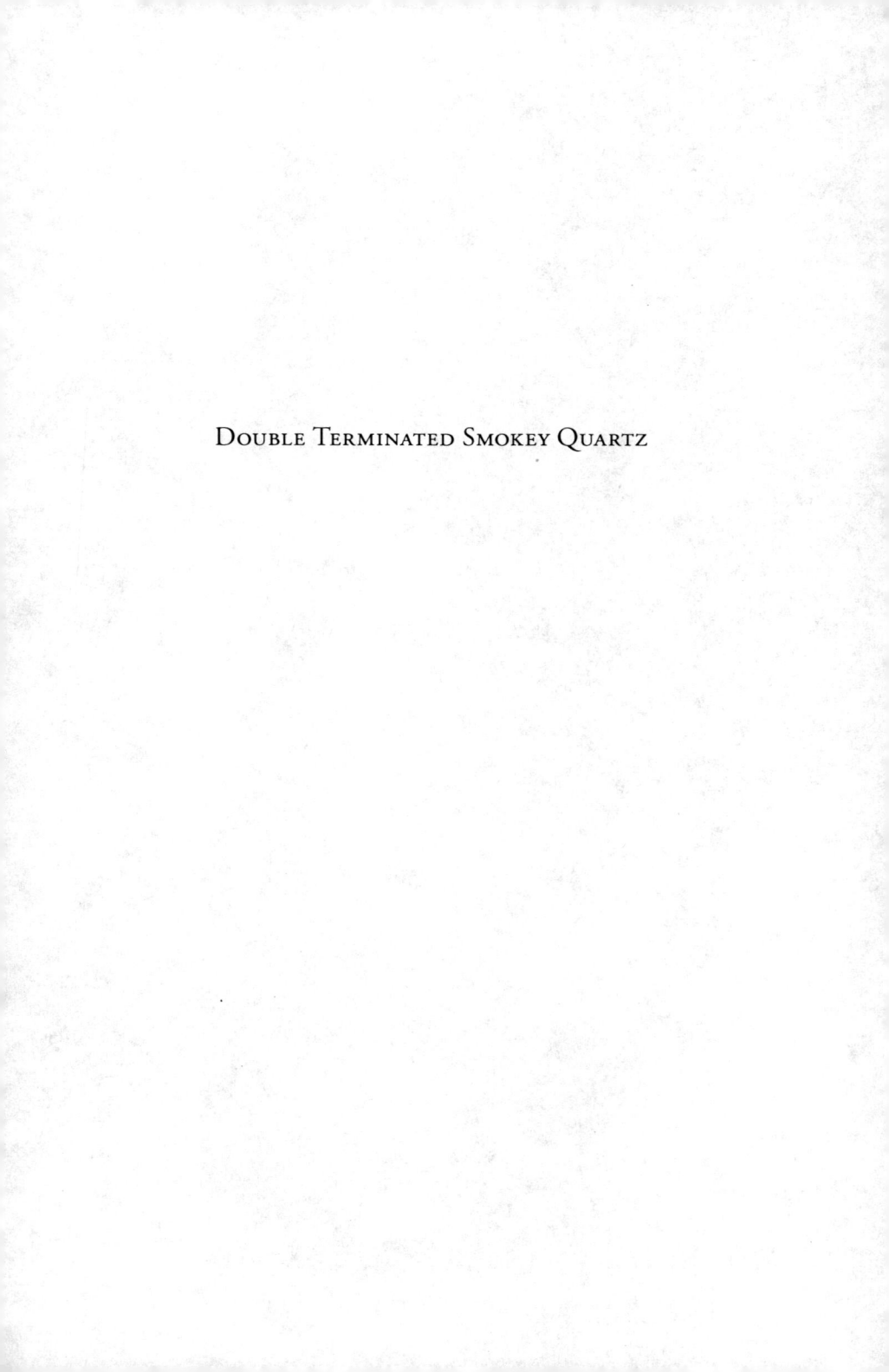

SHARPEN YOUR SENSES

ENERGY AWARENESS

There is a lot of evidence that ancient civilisations were more aware of energies than we are today. People in those early days were not only sensitive to the earth's energy, but also to healing energies of plant life and crystals. The many herbal remedies which we used to write off as 'old wives' tales are now being recognised as important ingredients in natural therapy and are being recommended by renowned herbalists.

As society became more demanding and materialistic, sensitivity faded into the background and was often denied or regarded as fanciful. Yet, throughout the ages, there has always been a 'sprinkling' of people maintaining energy sensitivity and natural healing know-how. These people were the true sages and were found amongst all nations. They were the healers, shamans and medicine men and women of the indigenous tribes. Mainly women, known as witches, often paid dearly with their lives while carrying out healing with crystals and/or herbs. Yet, during those dark days they were the ones who kept a bright stream of light alive with their beliefs and practices in the power of natural healing. They had the innate knowing that in future times this would be recognised as true spirituality and healing. These people intuitively knew of the bond between humans and crystals and their tremendous healing potential. Today, we once again recognise the energetic connection between crystals and humans and have access to instruments capable of measuring these energies.

In common with many sensitives, it is my personal belief that, at the present time, higher frequencies are increasingly entering the earth's atmosphere. These incoming energies are changing our planet and affect changes in our bodies and all living things on earth, including crystals! People who until recently were unaware of energy, are suddenly opening up and becoming conscious of subtle vibrations. Individuals who used to look upon crystals as pretty stones are discovering that there is more to them than just being beautiful and decorative. They actually can feel the energy in crystals.

With the increase in universal energy, there is an increase in the recognition of spiritual values. This creates a wonderful fertile environment for our crystal friends to make their official "comeback" and take an active part in their own evolutionary growth, while at the same time, crystals are assisting humankind in its renovation and helping to raise vibrations. In this way the entire planet, and all living beings on it, will reap the benefits.

CRYSTALS AND ENERGIES

A frequently asked question by my students is, "Why does one crystal have an energy you can hardly detect, while another similar one on the next shelf is pulsating with a strong crystal life force?"

Bearing in mind that crystals absorb energies, as well as radiate them, it begins to make some sense. If crystals are clean and clear, their energies are just lovely and when you hold that crystal in your hand, it feels good and so do you. On the other hand, if this crystal has been misused, or been in an area where unpleasant things have taken place, the crystal has absorbed these energies and consequently radiates these energies.

As a further illustration, consider the following scenario: A certain human being enjoys a healthy and happy lifestyle. This person is a positive chap and consequently it feels good to be in his vicinity because he radiates good, positive energies, which in turn affect you, and will make you feel good.

Compare this to somebody who has been deprived of the good things in life and, unless he happens to be a highly evolved soul, may well be depressed, resentful and 'down-in-the-dumps'. The energies this person radiates would not be the happiest. Spending some time in his company might well pull your energies down and you would no longer feel good, but more likely tired and in need of a good rest!

Something similar occurs in the case with crystals. Picture the following situation: In a certain geographical location is a vein with beautiful quartz crystals. These crystals are part and parcel of this 'vein' and have been growing gently for millennia, undisturbed in a peaceful environment, waiting for the day they may be of service. However, something unexpected happens above on the earth's surface. The humans living there disagree on some point or other and are unable to resolve their differences. Being 'human', the result of this is a vicious battle with much bloodshed, bitterness and vengeance. Whoever wins here is immaterial, but the negative energies thus created in this area will linger long after this battle has been fought and forgotten in human memory. The magnitude of this suffering has energetically saturated the entire battle area and its environment, including the soil and the crystals and all that lives within it. The peaceful and harmonious energies, which once were part of this area, have changed and the unhappy atmosphere thus created will linger and continue to haunt this place for a long time to come. Eventually, a natural cleansing will take place but, depending on its intensity, it may take hundreds of years or longer.

Some crystals do not have as nice an energy as their little friend on the next shelf because crystals absorb energies; regardless whether these are good or bad. In some cases, the sad consequences of the above-described incident are that the crystals, while still in the womb of Mother Earth, are detrimentally affected. Crystals are like sponges and absorb surrounding energies until they are completely saturated. The above imaginary 'incident' would affect the entire crystal vein with these dense unhappy energies. Crystals, which once were clear, become flooded with negativity.

Crystals can self-cleanse up to a point, given a clean and caring environment and a lot of time and patience. However, this is unlikely in the above scenario where the environment is as polluted as the poor crystals themselves. Unless some enlightened humans come to the aid of the area and cleanse it, it may well take hundreds of years, if not more, to clear the affected zone and the crystals from the trauma inflicted.

If you have ever visited one of those unfortunate places, and there are several in Britain, you need not be very sensitive to pick up on the distress and sadness still pervading the atmosphere in such environments, even though centuries have passed. Still fresh in my mind are places I have visited where severe battles took place, like Culloden and Salisbury.

I have personally been involved in 'clearing' a relatively small area, i.e. a large field in the Midlands. While attending a conference (and dressed to suit the important occasion) there were a couple of free hours in between sessions and some of us decided on a country tour. It started to rain, but what the heck, we felt safe in our car. While driving we passed through a particular area where all of us picked up on a strong, unhappy negativity, pervading the place. An enthusiast in our group knew the history of the place, which was purported to have been a battle area in Roman times. After some discussion (it was after all pelting with rain) it was jointly agreed we would try and clear this area.

Picture this small group of people, in their proverbial 'Sunday Best' in the middle of a muddy field, with rain lashing down, doing an impromptu ceremony. As we tuned into the energies we were aware of many unhappy soldiers in ancient battle dress, still haunting the place, being unable to leave it. We called upon and received assistance from the great Archangels and many, many other great Beings. Together we were able to 'help' the soldiers and finally succeeded in dissipating the negativity and bringing in the Light. When we finished, the rain stopped and a beautiful rainbow rewarded us!

It was at this point that we became aware of a line of cars parked on the side of the road, with curious drivers and passengers gazing and pointing towards us through their open windows, no doubt wondering what on earth these mad people were doing in the pouring rain in the middle of a field. As for us participants, although soaked to the skin, we experienced a wonderful feeling of satisfaction for clearing a little bit of Mother Earth.

Let us take a look at another scenario; another reason why some crystals are not feeling as good as some of their 'mates', although they may look very beautiful. We are once again in an area where some upheaval took place in the past although nothing quite as serious as the previous battleground, yet enough to have had an effect on the crystal vein below the ground. There is a sense of a less-than-happy atmosphere and very likely caused by the energy of the crystals below the surface. Hold on! Something is about to happen. An enterprising company discovers a rich crystal vein in the region. Totally unaware and insensitive to existing energies and not aware of past local history, they cannot wait to start 'harvesting' the crystals. Being in a hurry, they may well 'blast' their way through to gather their bounty as quickly as possible. This procedure is very distressing for crystals – just imagine being blasted to pieces after growing for thousands of years within the womb of Mother Earth.

Once the crystals have been mined, they are sorted by size and quality. Next these newly mined treasures are physically cleansed in a strong chemical; some are polished and faceted and will look very nice. Then the all important marketing process begins and the newly mined crystals are proudly displayed in the various sales venues. If we lived in an ideal world, these crystals should be given love, care and time to recuperate from their ordeal, but this time has not yet arrived.

The crystal lover, visiting the show or shop, may be captivated by these good looking specimen and be tempted to buy these crystals, unaware of the fact that these poor crystals are not yet able to supply positive energy, let alone be used for healing. The truth is that they may well be in need of healing themselves as they are still in a state of recovering from their 'explosive' birth trauma.

However being a sensitive purchaser you would 'feel' that these crystals are not ready for healing work but rather in need of healing. Should you acquire such a crystal, the best gift you could offer that crystal is to start treating it with love and reverence and cleanse it. Try one of the methods suggested in the 'Cleansing' chapter, but do not be surprised if you do not succeed immediately. These crystals need a lot of healing and time. The kindest thing you can do in this case is to return the crystal to Mother Earth for a while, asking her to clear and energise this crystal being. To safeguard your charge from disappearing to the far end of your garden, put the crystal in a large flowerpot filled with earth and, if possible, place the pot amongst plants and flowers in the garden, where it has the chance to recover. Leave your crystal there for a month or two before you check its 'condition', but do not be surprised if they want to stay there for longer. A great exercise for us humans in the lesson of 'patience'. The crystals have all the time in the world.

Once the crystal is clear, put it in a suitably quiet place in your home where it can spend time to recuperate from the trauma it has undergone in the process of coming to you. One of my best loved crystals spent two years 'resting' before he was able to get involved in healing work. If you come across such a crystal, please, spend some time with it hold it, stroke it and fill it with love. This will speed up the healing process and you will know when the time is right for this specially rescued crystal to start its 'work'. Your patience and care will be well rewarded because you will have created a special bond with this crystal. Together you will be able to work for the greater good of all, be it people, animal, or earth healing.

GOOD ENERGIES

The foregoing story illustrates the influence that the environment has on crystals while they are growing. However, as in life, nothing is completely black and white and there will be crystals from locations which only have been mildly affected, or been cleansed in the course of time. The energy of these crystals may not be as strong as you would like them to be. These crystals may not necessarily be able to do healing work immediately, but with love and care, they will regain their innate strong energy. Treasure these special beings and give them time. They have been through a traumatic experience and may be likened to humans who have suffered and grown as a result. Together with your energy, these crystals will be wonderful healers.

With so much going on in today's world, we tend to forget that there are many places on this planet of ours which have not been touched by negativity; areas where you find lovely, clear, and often healing energies. These are regions where growing crystals are bathed in love and light, as it was meant to be. You will often find these places in high altitudes where monasteries have created an aura of peace through meditation and prayer over the centuries. These may be places where holy people have lived, or where Mother Mary has appeared and people make pilgrimages coming from far and wide, such as Lourdes in France and Fatima in Portugal. A place that has not been touched by negativity simply may be a region where people have lived an uncomplicated peaceful life in keeping with nature.

On a more mundane level it does not necessarily follow that crystals can, or are, mined in these special areas. One particular place is Madagascar. Crystals originating from this island are very special. When one views these crystals they may not necessarily be the most physically appealing, but they have a wonderful deep healing energy.

Other places to find beautiful high energy crystals are Siberia and the Himalayas. Quite a few have been coming out of Russia in the recent past and some are breathtaking, both physically and energetically. Apart from these locations, there are other peaceful, but unknown places where truly good crystals are found. These crystals delight in assisting healers and are truly Light Workers. During their growth these crystals absorb the wonderful serenity and positive vibrations of their environment and if they are mined with care and respect, they become the special ones. These crystals enter the light of day with knowledge of their imminent task and need little, if any, coaching or prompting. These special beings will very likely tell you how and what you can do together for the benefit of humankind. Occasionally, such a crystal crosses your path. When it does, love and treasure it!

To sum up: When you wish to acquire crystals, take time and trouble to find the crystal you can work with (unless you simply shop for an ornament). It pays to 'look' beyond the surface. Hold the crystal in your left hand; sense it, 'feel' it and look 'into' it. If in doubt, use your pendulum and you will soon be given the answer. Your effort in choosing carefully will be well rewarded.

Note:
In the chapter of 'The Mystical Pendulum' in this book you will find helpful exercises about pendulum use, which will be helpful when choosing crystals.

SEEING' ENERGY

Since Crystal therapy is energy healing, it helps to be aware of the energy of the crystals with which you work. Learning to 'see' energy is really simple. As in learning to 'sense' energy, we can also (re)train ourselves to 'see' energies. This is not essential, but it is fun. There are several methods to achieve this, but one of the easiest, and in my opinion the quickest, is to start with nature in the great outdoors.

Ideally, choose a sunny or at least a bright day with no heavy overcast clouds. The best time to do this is before noon. Begin by finding yourself an outdoor spot where you feel comfortable and can totally relax. In most cases this may be your own garden, which is ideal, as it allows you to practise often. It does not matter whether your garden is large or small, as long as you have sight of at least a couple of large trees against a clear sky.

You also have the advantage that, in your own garden, you may well have a comfortable chair allowing you to completely relax. Alternatively, you may prefer to lie on your back on the lawn. Whatever you choose, be sure you have a good view of your chosen trees, as they are your practice 'tools'.

Once settled down comfortably and relaxed, connect to the

earth, either through your feet, or your body if you are lying on the grass. Open your eyes and for a short moment gaze at the blue sky. Next, let your eyes wander towards one of the big trees. Look at them but do not try to focus, just SEE the tree as part of the picture. After a little while move your vision towards the periphery of the branches and keep it there. Softly gaze. Do not try to see details, but suddenly, you will see lightness around the tree, following the shape of the branches. You may subconsciously blink, in order to focus and wonder if you really saw it. You did! But the moment you did blink, it disappeared. Now try again. This attempt may be somewhat easier. You have done it once and you know you can do it again. So repeat the process. With this second attempt you may well be able to hold the aura of the tree slightly longer.

Keep practising. Each time you do this, it becomes a bit easier. What a wonderful way to become more aware of the energies of the natural world and in the process revive your innate gift.

The energies of trees are at their strongest in the spring and early summer when the energy in the earth is high, encouraging growth of every kind. By the way, the winter is not a good time to start this exercise as the trees withdraw their energies into the earth. There is also a variation in energy amongst the trees. In my experience pine and oaks have a particularly strong energy and the aura can be seen more easily than in other trees.

If you continue this practice you should soon be able 'see' these energies and having learned the 'how to', you will now be able to extend this to your crystals. The principle is the same. To start with, choose a strong energy crystal, such as Madagascar or Himalayan Quartz, Russian Smokey Quartz, Selenite, Bloodstone, or Garnet. Initially it is best to place the crystal against a light, non-patterned background and follow the same procedure you used to see the tree's aura. With the practice you have already put in, it should be much easier.

Once having learned this, you will be able to determine the extent of energy of a particular crystal, which can be very useful when working with crystals as a healer. In addition, you will know when a crystal is happy and clean, as it will literally radiate its energy. When it has been working and collecting negativity, its normal brightness will turn dull. That is the time for a bath or another suitable cleanse. Once restored to cleanliness, your crystal will have regained its energy and radiant aura.

Being able to see the crystals' energies will greatly assist you when purchasing crystals and prevents you from making a wrong 'buy'. Those carrying a high energy usually sparkle and have a visible aura; obviously, not all crystals fall in this 'high energy' category, and that is fine. You would not want to use these high energy beings all the time. Remember the purpose you are buying your crystal for. When working with it for healing, there are occasions when a lesser energy may be called for and that particular crystal may just be the right one.

Seeing a crystal's energy field also helps in circumstances when you are attracted to a crystal, which, physically, may not be the most enticing specimen, yet it has a lovely aura. These are often crystals which have been damaged during mining, or been handled carelessly or roughly. In spite of this (or more correctly because of it) they have a special radiance. Like people who have suffered, they too have overcome their trauma and in many cases have a special energy. If you are attracted to such a crystal, do not hesitate to buy it. Love it and treasure it. These crystals are great natural healers. For years I have been working with lovely Madagascar Quartz. Lovely in my eyes, but somebody wanting to purchase a similar crystal would not look at it twice. Yet, it has been one of the most important healers in my collection.

When you are able to 'see' a crystal's energy field it can prevent you from making wrong purchases. You may come across a nice looking crystal in a shop but it does not look or feel good energetically. Your first impulse may be that you want to 'rescue' it, to take it home to care and restore it. If you are like me, you will feel sorry for it and may buy it nevertheless. You will take it home and try to cleanse and revive it. Great! Have a go! However, do not be disappointed if your crystal does not respond. Sadly, we have to accept that not all crystals can be completely restored. If they come from a highly polluted area, they may have absorbed so much negative and dense energies that it is nearly impossible to cleanse and restore them completely. Some crystals may take years to shed this negativity.

However, in the odd case, you may be successful with a lot of T.L.C. and patience, but if this does not produce the desired results, thank the crystal for the service it has given in the past and bury it with honour and blessings in your garden where in due course it will be healed by Mother Earth.

SENSING CRYSTALS

If you truly want to work with and connect to the Crystal Kingdom it helps if you are sensitive to crystal energies. If you have not tried to ascertain your sensitivity to crystals, or are unaware how to do this, do not worry. Everybody is more sensitive than they think. This process can be learned and the suggestions in this book should help you to make a start.

'Sensing' is best explained as a personal experience; your unique awareness of the properties and effects of a specific crystal. This is a helpful attribute for everybody who wishes to work with crystals, but it is even more important for Crystal Therapists since they need to be aware of the true energies of the crystals when using them in a healing session. Sensing energies of crystals therefore, is a very important part of learning for those doing the crystal course. Naturally, everyone can do research and look up individual properties officially attributed to a particular crystal in one of the many reference books on sale. However, this can be very perplexing, especially for a novice working with crystals. Many books give different interpretations about the same crystal, which only adds to confusion. Up until now you may well have considered this information was the answer to choosing your crystals. Not quite so.

Too much mixed information exists about the 'properties' of crystals, especially how to use them for specific conditions. The general impression is, for instance, that you simply place a Rosequartz on the heart chakra to heal heartaches and pains, be it physical or emotional. But surprise, surprise; it did not quite do the job. Would it be that simple. Crystal healing does not work that way.

If you seriously want to work as a crystal healer, it is necessary to have a strong personal connection and in-depth knowledge of each of the crystals you will be using in your healing work. The best way to achieve this is to attend a two year accredited crystal therapy training course. As you gain more knowledge about crystals you will appreciate the necessity of a thorough training, which is essential and very rewarding. However this is not everybody's path and that is what this book is all about, giving you an understanding and pointers of how to use them for yourself in the best possible way. As a crystal lover you will actually find you enjoy the experience of getting to know your individual crystals. They are like any friend; to truly love them you have to get to know them first and, in the case of crystals, sensing their energies is a good start.

In our classes in the Vantol College we practise 'group sensing'. Being part of a group of like-minded individuals creates a strong energy, and this makes sensing a lot easier for its participants. When we start practising, every one holds an identical crystal in the palm of their left hand with their right hand loosely cupped over it. Together we go into a meditative state and everyone allows feelings, thoughts or other sensations to come to them. In a way, you, the sensors, are just observers and watch what happens.

To new students it is often a surprise that everybody receives information in a way unique to them. Some students will 'see' pictures, others will get strong feelings in their body, yet others may hear words describing some qualities of the crystal they are holding. The interesting thing is that, when sharing information after the sensing, there is an overall common thread of the crystal's properties.

The different ways this information is communicated is

fascinating. Let me tell you about one of my special students. The moment we began the sensing meditation, she started 'travelling' with one of her 'animal companions'. This was often an eagle, an owl or a zebra, and the animal would take her to some special place deep into the earth to show and tell her about the physical and spiritual properties of the crystal she was holding.

Another student during these sensing meditations would invariably go into a pyramid, where she would be taken to a special room with a brilliant light (each visit with a different colour) and receive information on a ticker tape.

Other students have felt effects in specific parts of their bodies. They would know whether the particular crystal worked more efficiently on the spiritual, rather than on the physical bodies, and visa-versa.

During one lesson we were sensing Snowflake Obsidian. Everybody loved it and felt nice and calm, except one student. She put (or rather 'threw') her crystal on the floor as though a bee had stung her! The moment she held it she experienced quite a violent headache. It was not a nice experience for the student in question, but a great lesson for the class, indicating that at no time can you assume that a particular crystal will give a similar reaction to every client.

In another class an incident occurred while the students were sensing Haematite. Discussing the crystal's merits afterwards, most of the students complained of a headache (which disappeared the moment they put the crystal down). Yet, there was one woman wearing a big Haematite bracelet, announcing that it felt lovely and she could not bear leaving the house without it as it made her feel so good. These experiences show that there are no hard and fast rules. This woman clearly craved the energy Haematite had to offer, whereas for all the others it was an energy not compatible with theirs. The way each person responds to the energies of individual crystals can be very different.

The above classroom experiences confirm that there are people with an intuitive aversion to certain crystals, which others may love. Amongst the latter are people who love their crystal so much that they carry it with them at all times, as they cannot bear to be without this treasure.

Just to show that these illustrations tell us nothing 'new', I will tell you a little tale from medieval times. It was believed by many that precious gems and crystals had their own sense (energy) and reacted to individual people (human energies) in a certain way. A legend exists about a certain bishop by the name of St. Martial, who wore very special gloves, which were studded with exquisite gems. These crystals were purported to be so sensitive that, when an act of sacrilege occurred before the saint, these crystals were so shocked that they leapt from their settings in front of the horrified bystanders! Perhaps the story of this excessive reaction of the crystals may have gathered momentum over the years, but it points out the belief in crystal and human synergy. To me, the above tale indicates that St. Martial's personal abhorrence of the sacrilege created the energy, which affected the crystals.

Our personal feelings have a very strong effect on our energies and Crystal therapists are well aware of this. They know that each client has his or her personal energy pattern, but so has she herself, and so have the crystals she will be using in the healing session. Put these three elements together and you have a unique energy pattern. With this in mind, it is easy to understand why each healing requires a very unique approach with carefully individually chosen crystals.

To illustrate this, let us look at an imaginary situation:

A lady is visiting a Crystal Therapist for a treatment. We call her Helen. This person is unique and so are her energies. Helen is different from everybody else. The therapist too, is an individual and the energy she channels is equally exclusive. Finally, there is an array of beautiful healing crystals to choose from, eager to go to 'work', each one with a different vibration. Yet, within this triangle of energies, the therapist has to create the ideal healing synergy to help Helen.

In a simple way this story explains how the skill and sensitivity of an experienced therapist are essential if an effective treatment is to be achieved.

These days many so called 'chakra sets' are offered for sale, i.e. crystals in keeping with the chakra colours, but these 'uniform energies' are not necessarily ideal for you, or your client. Remember, Helen is unique, and so is every one of you reading this book. Your energetic needs are exclusive and the crystals applied to you in a healing session have to be just the right match to balance your energies at that particular time. On the face of it our crystal therapist has a complicated choice to make but, if properly qualified, her two-year training has prepared her to make the right decisions and she will know how to give Helen the treatment she needs, with crystals chosen exclusively for her condition.

Practical sensing

You can help prepare yourself in the sensing game by focussing your energies. Our body has a very finely inbuilt antenna, which continuously picks up energies from our environment on a subconscious level. To become consciously aware of this, you will find it helps when you are completely relaxed in body and mind while holding a vibrant crystal in your hands. Be aware of the crystal you hold, i.e. focus on that to the exclusion of everything else, in this way it will become very easy to 'pick up' its vibrations. Do not try too hard as this will hold you back.

Take as an example an imaginary telephone conversation on your mobile to a friend in the midst of a rowdy party. Yet, you choose to only hear your friend's voice and mentally block out all other sounds.

As a flautist you attend a concert but only 'hear' the flute part when listening to Mozart's Flute Concerto, 'filtering out' all other instruments.

The same is the case when you are sensing a crystal; when you 'tune in' you are aware only of the energies of the crystal now in your hand.

Sensing crystals is something everybody can achieve. Start by choosing a particular crystal to which you are attracted and make sure it is 'squeaky clean'. Find a peaceful spot and go into a meditative state, place the chosen crystal in the palm of your left hand, which is resting in your lap. Loosely cup your right hand over it, while remaining totally relaxed and clearing your mind of all extraneous thoughts. Be an observer! Be alert to possible feelings in your body, some unexpected thoughts which may flash into your mind; perhaps you see colours or you may 'see' places or pictures, or 'sense' angelic beings. Whatever comes up, remember it and when you come out of your meditation write down your feelings and impressions immediately.

It may happen that you do not feel or sense anything the first couple of times, but please persevere, sensing with the same crystal several times over. Rome was not build in one day; neither can you expect your sensing gift, having been dormant to date, to suddenly 'jump' into action! Be gentle with yourself and give yourself time. The crystal's energy will work on you whether you feel it or not, but you might feel lighter, or perhaps more balanced.

Something has happened. Sensing is a very worthwhile exercise. Not only does it strengthen your connection to the crystal kingdom, but it is also a wonderful tool, which can help you develop your sensitivity and quicken your personal transformation.

****

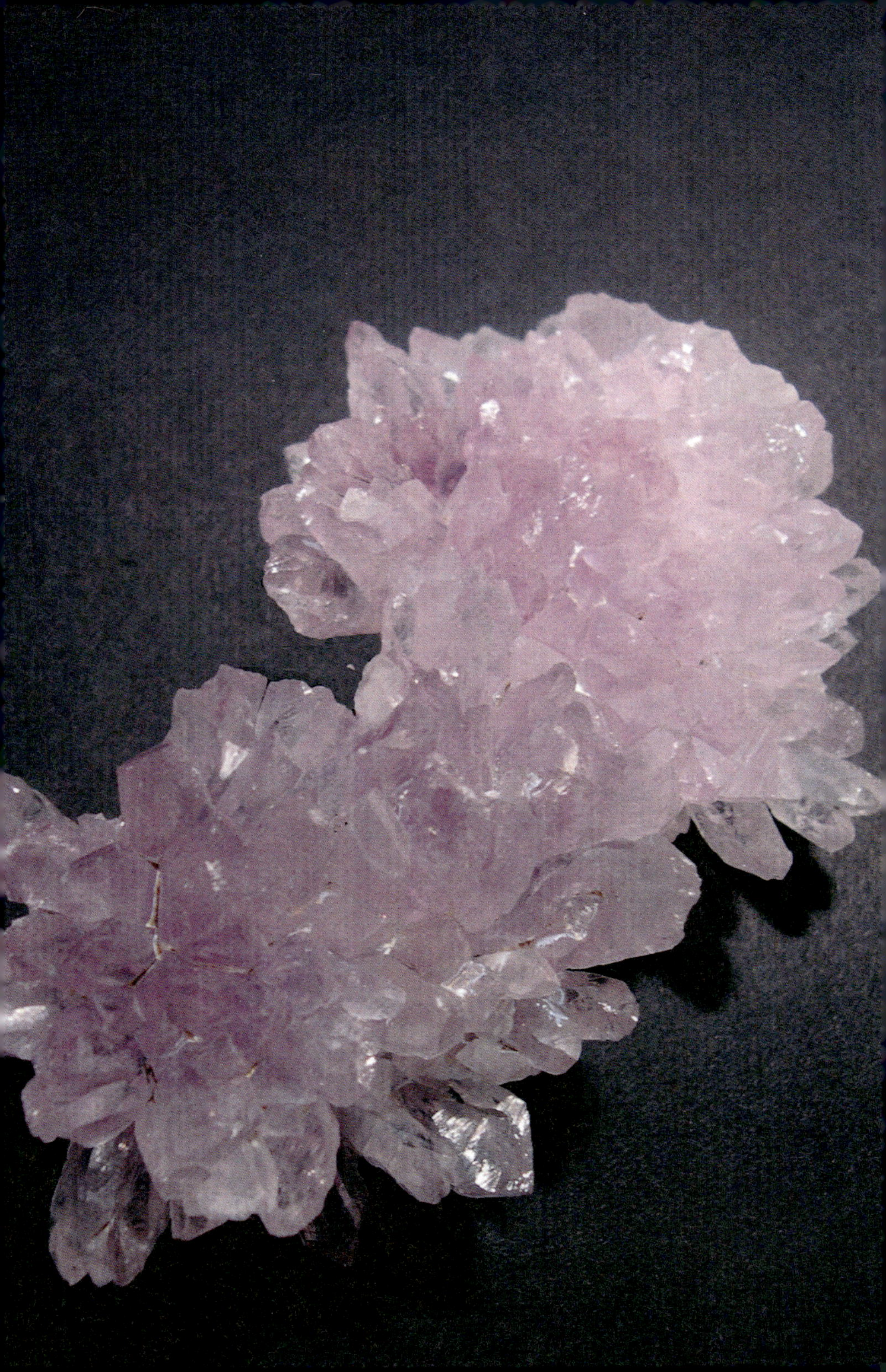

AMETHYST ROSETTES

USING CRYSTAL POWER

PROTECTION WITH CRYSTALS

What does protection have to do with crystals? What kind of protection and why crystals?

In today's turbulent world we are subjected to much undesirable energies, which comes from a variety of sources. It is impossible to ignore the fact that we live in a technologically advanced age and are surrounded by electronic equipment, wherever we find ourselves. This includes computers, at work and at home, microwaves and music centres. A mobile phone is a must for each of us, not to mention our individual electronic aids like a portable iPOD, MP4 or CD player, a laptop or palmtop. If we are lucky, we do not live under a pylon supporting high-tension electrical wires, which might add further harmful energies. In short we are surrounded, even bombarded, by energy from the moment our electronic alarm wakes us up in the morning, until we snuggle under our electric blanket at night. We literally live in a sea of electronic waves and know it or not, our bodies are constantly subjected to an excess of electronic waves. While we enjoy the comfort and convenience of our sophisticated equipment, its energy does not necessarily contribute to our daily health regime.

Although we are a resilient species, no one can say for certain how this new energy will affect our bodies in the long term. So far it has been reported that the effect of this excessive electronic bombardment manifests in different ways, such as extreme tiredness, constant headaches, loss of memory, skin complaints and many different allergies. These symptoms can be felt strongly by office workers who see little daylight and work with computers and other electronic office equipment under artificial light, not to mention harmful leylines.

Neither are we exempt in the home. A look in the average kitchen is quite interesting. A microwave oven is considered indispensable, as are other domestic paraphernalia. I remember having acquired an early microwave, which, my friends told me, was a 'must have' for my busy life. Unfortunately being of a sensitive nature, I could feel the (ill)effects of this new miracle equipment to such an extend that neither my daughters, nor myself, could bear the thing in our kitchen and, although almost new, we carted it off to the refuse centre and to this day I cook in the old fashioned oven.

Protection from Equipment

We have to accept the fact that we are living in an 'electronic age' and accept that these energies are with us and all around us. It is now generally acknowledged that they do have a detrimental effect on our well-being. Fortunately there are ways and means to protect ourselves. Several practical 'tools' have been developed to counteract the harmful effect of these energies and you will find an assortment on stands of the Body, Mind and Spirit Exhibitions. Most come in the forms of pendants, often made from different kinds of exotic metal that have undergone specialised processes. The buyer is told that these items will either reflect or neutralise these harmful energies. In most cases they do an efficient job, but can be quite costly. However, there is no need to spend a fortune. Do you realise that you can achieve the same effect with certain crystals?

Protection from Computers with Black Tourmaline

It is now generally acknowledged, and much reported in the press, that 'Electronic Smog' i.e. invisible emissions from mobile phones, power cables, electrical appliances, microwaves, computers etc may have a detrimental affect on the human system. The author also holds this view. Symptoms of this electronic invasion include head-aches, feeling exceedingly tired, some people find it difficult to concentrate on their work in this environment and others even prefer to forego computers and revert to the now ancient art of hand-writing.

Much confusion exists about the use of crystals for protection from Electronic Smog. Several students who take our courses find this computer energy too much to cope with, until... they find out about Black Tourmaline. Equally, new students tell me they need not worry because they protect themselves from these energy waves by putting a Rosequartz, Moonstone or Blue Lace Agate between themselves and their computer. My involuntary reaction is 'Poor things!' (Obviously referring to the relevant Rosequartz, Moonstone or Blue Lace). The reason for this reaction is because these crystals have a gentle energy and this electronic smog is too much for them. They may possibly protect you for one or two days, but sadly, during these few days they give their all, trying to carry out a task that is beyond them; a too heavy a load for these gentle beings. All too soon these crystals have no energy left to counteract this particular energy and they literally collapse. The sad thing is they can no longer help you either. They will often break or shatter or, when holding them, simply feel what I call 'dead'. They have little or no energy left to recover. The kindest thing you can do in these circumstances is bury them and ask Mother Earth to heal them in time.

When asked where this information came from, it is usually some 'knowledgeable' friend who has attended a weekend seminar. Alas, this friend has been miss-informed. Yes, 'it' will work for a couple of days, but at the cost of the poor crystal.. The fact is that very few crystals are strong enough to carry out this Protection Job and yet maintain an active 'life span'.

One of the very few crystals able to tackle this job efficiently is Black Tourmaline. Tourmaline is the Knight of the Crystal Kingdom. These crystals can annihilate harmful emissions coming from your computer.. You may have to search around a little to find one since it is not a crystal you purchase to decorate your home with and therefore easy to locate. Your best chances of finding them are at Crystal Exhibitions, which regularly take place throughout the UK, Europe and the US, and are well advertised.

If you are someone who does a lot of computer work, it is worthwhile investing in a reasonably sized Black Tourmaline, maybe one roughly two or more inches long and one inch in diameter. Place this between your computer and yourself and you will be well protected from harmful emissions from your computer. It is essential though to take good care of your protective Black Tourmaline friend and you can do this by giving it a good cleanse every couple of weeks by placing it overnight in water with a couple of drops of Crab Apple Flower Remedy[11]♦ and your Black Tourmaline will protect you for years to come.

However, if this crystal is worked hard, it will begin to show signs of wear and tear after four or five years. A few bits of white chalk-like substance will occur in its striations. The change from black to white occurs very, very gradually, but as long as the greater part of your Black Tourmaline remains black, it will work efficiently. If, after ten or so years, the 'white bits' have taken over, thank your Tourmaline for its service and return it to Mother Earth by burying it in a happy energy spot.

If you have a lot of electronic equipment in your home, you might also like to spend a little more money on smaller pieces of Black Tourmaline of about one to two inches long and place them on your TV, music centre, Microwave etc. This gives you all round protection from negative waves in your home.

---

11 ♦ One of Dr. Bach 38 Remedies, based on single wild flowers and tree blossoms.

Personal Protection with Sodalite

Being aware of energies is, on the whole, a blessing. It allows you to sense the energies of crystals, flowers and everything that is alive around you. This awareness may extend to your environment and to the people in your life. All this is great, provided these energies are of a positive nature. If you belong to this sensitive group of people, you may sense and feel very uncomfortable when somebody is upset or angry in your environment, even if it is not directed towards you.

As an example, you could liken a human being to a mobile phone. When carrying on a conversation it broadcasts the energies of the person's voice through the ether. The same thing happens to our thoughts. Although not spoken, the stronger the feelings behind the emotions, the stronger the energy radiating from that 'personal broadcast'. Like the mobile phone, this will be received by the person to whom these energies are directed and if they are less then flattering, the recipient may sense them in an uncomfortable way. If this is an isolated case, we can cope with it and no harm is done. However, if the sender carries out a vendetta against somebody, it will become increasingly unpleasant for the recipient and there is a definite need for Personal Protection.

If Black Tourmaline is the crystal to protect us from computer and microwave emissions, then Sodalite has been delegated the People Protector. Sodalite is another stone, which a novice crystal enthusiast might not give a second glance. After all, it is plain looking and unassuming. Yet Sodalite has a tremendous amount to offer. It is 'the' great protector against negative energies from human origin and offers protection to those of us working in a crowded environment. This may be a busy office or shop, filled with many people, each one trying to cope with their own life's challenges and subsequent tensions.

Furthermore, a lot of Geopathic stress is often present in our over-crowded cities and whether you are aware of its origin or not, it affects you and everyone else. Add to this the fact of someone working in a busy office, where tempers may well run short.... The inevitable outcome is an atmosphere brimming with negative energies. So what can you, as an individual, do about this? Finding another job in more congenial surroundings would be great, but this is not always feasible. Therefore, if you are unfortunate enough to hold a job in that type of environment, you need protection to remain unaffected from the negativity and the discomfort it causes. This is where Sodalite can be your ally and make life in difficult environments tolerable.

There are many forms of Sodalite available, all of which can be used for protection. In fact we are spoilt for choice. You could go for the simple Sodalite tumblestone but, if you have the opportunity of purchasing a string of Sodalite beads, (preferably little spheres) don't hesitate. They are a worthwhile investment. This spherical shape is the most effective as it will absorb energy from all around, transform it and send out cleansed energy in equal measure.

My next choice would be to go for the humble tumblestones. They are very reasonably priced; invest in a dozen or so. You can put some in your pocket; around or on your desk at work and exchange them every day for 'fresh' ones.

Because Sodalite is a hard working crystal, your necklace and/or tumblestones need regular cleansing. The frequency of cleansing depends on the existing situation. If you are unlucky to work in a truly challenging environment, this may need to be carried out daily. If this is not the case, you may get away with a few days grace or do a weekly cleanse. All the same, it is important to check if your Sodalite is clear on a daily basis. Use your faithful pendulum to make sure your Sodalite is still clear. Only then can it give you the best possible protection.

The simplest and best method for cleansing Sodalite is placing them in water overnight, to which a few drops of Crab Apple flower essences have been added. However in the case of a necklace it might be preferable to cleanse this in incense and finish by giving it a gentle rub with a soft cloth. Too much bathing might harm the lovely shine it has.

In short, Sodalite is a not-to-be-without crystal. Luckily it is modestly price and the crystal shops usually have a good supply!

****

CRYSTAL MANDALAS

A Mandala symbolises a safe refuge of inner reconciliation and wholeness
- Carl Jung

What is a mandala?

To many people the word 'Mandala' conjures up a mystical picture. I remember first hearing this word many, many moons ago and vaguely felt there was a connection to far Eastern images. The Sanskrit definition of a Mandala is a picture (mostly) in a circular design that radiates from a central point or dot. Although not all Mandalas are circular, the circle is the most common form. The picture itself can be anything; simple or complicated, but often has a spiritual theme. Their origin can be traced back to the beginning of recorded history. Mandalas always have been considered sacred and powerful objects. In Tibetan culture mandalas were represented as patterns of creation; an integrated structure organised around a unifying centre. It was considered a cosmic diagram, reminding us of our relationship with the Infinite.

What is its purpose?

I first became seriously interested in mandalas after initially getting to know the Crystal Kingdom. Wow. I was so excited! Here was another means of working with crystals for the greater good, yet in a different way. Upon study and tentative practise of this newly acquired skill, I was bowled over by the energy that could be accessed and applied for healing and positive purposes. I had to know more.

The first thing I learned was that it is important to choose a specific purpose when creating a mandala. Once its intention is established, one must focus one hundred per cent on this intention while physically creating the mandala.

Therefore, you have to decide the kind of mandala you want to make and which kind would be best for your purpose before you begin your work. The choices for dedicating this strong energy are as numerous as there are different kinds of mandalas and intentions.

The obvious dedication that immediately comes to my mind as a therapist is "healing". This may be for self or others. It can also be very effective for distant healing on people, animals or specific situations, such as earth upheavals or other traumatic events. In classes in the Vantol College, we often create a mandala for planetary healing which creates a powerfully effective energy that is strongly felt by all its participants. Another valuable intention is for self development or meditation. Creating a mandala can have a very relaxing and calming effect on the mind as well as on the body especially in times of stress.

The above mentioned intentions are a few among many, many others. During our journey in this lifetime, we are constantly faced with unexpected challenges. It is in times like these that it is good to know there are ways in which we can help ourselves to deal with challenges and turn them into tools for growth. By making mandalas, we create something beautiful and something unique which is specifically ours. This gives us one more method to help us to cope and overcome personal challenges.

TYPES OF MANDALA

SAND MANDALA.

There are many different ways in which mandalas can be created. We could consider the birth place of mandalas to be Tibet and it is the sand mandala which has been created and applied by monks as long as can be remembered. They are the most amazingly complicated sand mandala pictures. To the monks it is not a matter of putting a design together, but it is a sacred ceremony, a tradition which has been observed for hundreds of years. This makes sense when we understand that Mandalas are seen as a powerful focus for devotion and meditation when the designs created for mandalas are considered as a representation of the spiritual universe.

Sand paintings are not the prerogative of the Tibetans as they have been found in India, other Eastern countries, and amongst North American native cultures. But as the Tibetan sand mandalas are probably the largest and best known, let us take a closer look at 'how' these most beautiful mandalas are created by the Tibetan monks.

Before starting the physical labour of making the mandala, the monks meditate for days, or even weeks. Once they have decided on a theme, they create its design together and start by making drawings of the intended depiction. This is important considering that the actual mandala can often be as large as 2 meters in diameter. Understandably, this is a phenomenal task. Colouring the sand in the chosen hues comes next. When the time is finally right for the mandala to be created with the coloured sand, it is done by several monks working together as a team. A mandala always starts from the centre and the pattern is created moving outwards. The sand is carefully applied through small funnels and, depending on the size of the design, completion may take many weeks.

Once finished, the monks will activate their mandala with prayer and chant. They dedicate it for its intended purpose, followed by further meditation on it, thus creating a powerful energy directed towards their chosen purpose. Having accomplished this, their mission is completed and the beautiful mandala, which has taken so much energy and effort to create on the part of the monks, is swept away and dispersed in the winds, or it is allowed to flow away in water.

To people from the West, this seems close to sacrilege, but to understand this we need to know a bit more about the Tibetan philosophy. This action emphasises the message that everything on earth is of a passing nature, and that we should not be attached to anything in this lifetime which is a mere speck in the vastness of time. After all, the intention for which this mandala was created has served its purpose and the energy, focussed on a particular purpose, will continue to work for the highest good as long as needed.

Drawn Mandalas

When you were young were you ever fascinated by the patterns in a kaleidoscope? I remember trying to create similar coloured drawings in a circle, simply because they were so lovely and intriguing. With hindsight I feel that there has to be a far memory in the human psyche about patterns in a circle that have a deep esoteric meaning. This memory is something of which we are not consciously aware, but is part of us.

Mandalas are very individual. They can be scientific, intricate or simple. Whatever design or materials used, they represent the energy of the 'maker'. It is important to be aware of the intent that goes into the creation of a mandala. Therefore, it is less important to be concerned with how it is made or what materials are used. A simple mandala, made with sincere and positive intention, is as effective as any intricate pattern.

Hildegard von Bingen made some of the best samples of drawn mandalas. Hildegard, as mentioned earlier had great talent. She was a great artist as well as being a writer and musician and used her creativity to produce some of the most beautiful and intricate mandalas, although they were not always in the shape of a circle.

Most have a religious theme showing the most delicate drawings and beautiful colour combinations. Samples of it can be viewed on many websites and in books.

CROP CIRCLE MANDALAS

The Crop Circle phenomenon is very much older than most of us are aware. As the origin of those who created them has not been established, crop circles have a particularly mysterious attraction. In recent years, thousands of crop circles have been reported all over the world. They mainly appeared overnight in corn, wheat or other grain fields. The patterns of these crop circles are varied and range from simple to immeasurably beautiful and complex creations.

Research has and is being conducted by both the military establishment and numerous individuals. The military and scientific community are keen to explain the circles as hoaxes, which in some cases may be true. However, amongst other explanations, we are told that they have been created by an extraterrestrial source, nature spirits, whirlwind or friction. Undoubtedly, we shall find out one day, but it is intriguing to see the Sacred Geometry in all its diversity which appears within mandala shapes. Sacred Geometry consists of universal symbols which emit certain cosmic energies. These patterns are as ancient as humanity and transcend religions. Sacred geometry has been found in pagan temples, Christian churches, Islamic mosques, tabernacles of Jehovah and in shrines of martyrs.

The earliest known crop circle was recorded in 1647. I have been told that there is a carving in existence to confirm this. It is a fair assumption that this must have been one of the many that appeared in those days. In our time, awareness of crop circles first gained public awareness in 1972. Since then, increased appearances of crop circles continue to attract public interest, as well as never ceasing speculations about their origins. Being the healthy curious humans we are, we would like to know the answer, but in this book we are not concerned who created them. What is of interest to us is that the most common shape, the various patterns within the circle, are often forms of known Sacred Geometry, and as such 'broadcast' a specific energy into the environment. It is interesting to note that an increasing number of sightings are appearing at this time of great changes, both environmental and personal. Changes are essential when growth of any kind takes place and in my opinion, the establishment of these wonderful 'crop-mandalas' are confirmation of caring unseen forces, creating a particular energy to help us ease into the new era just around the corner.

From friends who have 'walked' these circles shortly after their creation, I have learned that the energy from these 'earth mandalas' is so amazing that it has to be experienced. It is said to have a beneficial holistic influence on the human body, mind and undoubtedly on the environment.

If you are interested and have a moment, do take a look at the many crop circle galleries shown on the website. You will see some of many intriguing, as well as familiar patterns.

CRYSTAL MANDALAS

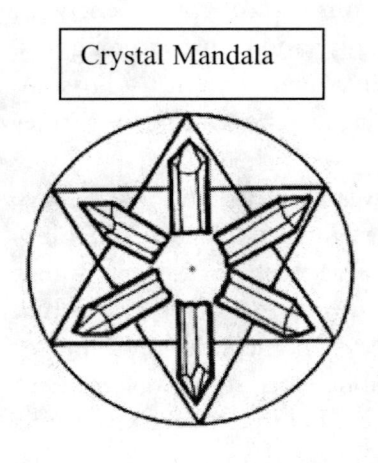

Crystal Mandala

There are numerous materials you could use to create a mandala, but making a mandala with objects you love and with which you feel happy increases its energy manifold. Obviously, the principle would be similar if you used other materials such as feathers or flowers, but crystals with their amazing innate energy are an ideal means of creating a high vibrational, effective mandala. Thus, by choosing to create your mandala with crystals adds considerably to the mandala's energy.

At this point I can almost hear the question, *"Which crystals do I use?"* The reply is straightforward: you can use any kind of crystal you feel you want to place into your mandala. It is nice to have a special, perhaps large, crystal in the centre, one which has meaning for you, or one toward which you feel particularly fond. Obviously, if you set up a mandala to help you meditate, you would not use grounding crystals, such as Black Tourmaline, Hematite or Red Jasper. However, if you have a close connection with the Crystal Kingdom, you may be inspired to choose certain crystals you are drawn to at that particular moment. These could be crystals chosen intuitively, or with the knowledge you have about them. You may feel you want to set up a mandala with one particular crystal, such as Rosequartz, with the intention to spread love, and that is fine. The choice and intention are entirely yours. There is no need to rush out and buy some exquisite gems to create a mandala. The humble tumble stones are great and very practical for this purpose. Perhaps you have a large selection of natural, rough crystals, or some lovely faceted ones. All of these can be mixed and are perfect for creating an effective mandala!

CREATING A MANDALA

The fore-going gives you an overview of what mandalas are and how they can be used for healing or act as 'personal helpers'. Have you ever attempted or felt you wanted to make a mandala yourself? If not, how about creating your personal mandala? Perhaps you may have made one in the past when you were part of a group. Creating a mandala with a group is a valuable experience, because the joint energy and mutual intention contributes much to its effect, but in everyday life it is not always feasible to do this in group context. Furthermore, you may want to make a mandala in private with your own specific intention. Your creation could be for any of the intentions mentioned earlier in this chapter, or for a purpose taken

from the list below.
- As an aid to meditation
- As part of spiritual practice
- For physical healing
- For personal growth
- For cleansing and protecting living environments
- For earth healing
- To heal relationships
- To assist in working through a personal problem
- As a method of manifestation

CREATING YOUR OWN CRYSTAL MANDALA

There are many methods and rituals that revolve around creating a mandala, but the following one is straightforward and used by the Vantol College. It easy as well as very effective:

1. Before starting the ritual, meditate on your intention for this mandala and having made a decision, clearly state this; write it down or, whenever possible, make an affirmation out loud.

2. You can draw the pattern you have in your mind on a clean piece of white paper and then translate this into your crystal mandala: This allows you to choose and prepare your crystals in advance. By creating an outline for your mandala, you add power to your intention; alternatively you could decide to create your mandala intuitively as you go along.

3. Cleanse and dedicate the crystals you are going to use.

4. * Energetically cleanse and bless the intended area; * Spread a clean white cloth on the floor; * Light a candle and incense stick and ask your Angelic helpers to bring blessings onto this spot and the procedure.

5. You are now ready to start the physical creation of your mandala. It is important to always begin by placing your chosen major crystal in the centre; i.e. always work from the centre outwards and continue this way to create your chosen pattern. Whilst doing this, take your time and continue to focus your mind on your purpose. It is normal to get distracted every so often, but as soon as you realise this, re-focus your mind on the creation and purpose of your mandala.

6. When your mandala is complete, activate it. You do this by once again invoking your angelic helpers, together blessing it and re-affirming the intention for its creation. Then relax and meditate on the purpose of your newly created mandala, absorb the beautiful energy and enjoy its beauty.

7. When you have finished your meditation, ask the Angelic Kingdom that the energy created may remain active as long as needed in the etheric realms and, when its purpose has been achieved, to disperse the energy.

8. Gently remove the crystals, starting from the outside in, leaving your Central Crystal till last.

9. Thank your crystals for the energy they have shared.

10. Cleanse the area where the mandala was built with sound or incense.

11. Ground yourself in the usual manner.

Every time you create a mandala in the manner described above, or in a similar way, you help yourself or others by assisting with a certain situation. In addition, together with the chosen crystals, you create a valuable energetic contribution to the well-being of humanity, our planet and beyond.

CRYSTALS AND MEDITATION

For many of you reading this book, meditating is an integral part of daily life. Your reasons for doing this vary; perhaps you do it to make progress on the spiritual path; perhaps you do it to gain strength to cope with the pressures of every day life, or simply for relaxation. There are many ways to meditate and we choose whichever method feels right for us and suits our life style. At the same time it is good to be aware of the value of regular meditation practice. Some of these benefits are:

- It helps you relax
- It facilitates connecting you to your true self
- It helps to 'see' situations or circumstances in a more realistic light, thus allowing you to better deal with them.

Most of you reading this book are aware of the importance of regular meditation practice and, in the unlikely case you should forget, there is always the 'new age' media to remind you of its importance. Whatever your reason for meditating, my personal experience is that, when practised regularly, it definitely helps to keep one relaxed and on an 'even keel'.

As a person who loves crystals, meditating with these beautiful beings adds a further dimension to your meditations. You will already know from a previous chapter that crystals amplify energies and this is exactly what happens when you meditate with a crystal which is appropriate for you at this moment in time.

If you meditate with spiritual intentions, the right crystal will help you to relax and connect to Higher Energies more easily and quickly. Living in the turbulent times we do, and the many demands made on us daily, create a lot of stress, it can be hard to let go of those endless worrying thoughts whirling through our minds. Simply holding a carefully chosen crystal in your hands can be very calming and soothing. It helps to relax your physical body and floods your mind with peaceful energies. Once your body has been saturated, this energy will extend to your subtle bodies and before you know it you will find yourself enveloped in a cocoon of soothing, calming energies.

CHOOSING THE RIGHT CRYSTAL

Our spiritual, emotional and energetic needs vary from day to day and to choose an appropriate crystal for your meditation depends largely on your needs of the moment, i.e. what is happening in your life and environment and your reactions to this. It is well known that emotions and circumstances affect both mind and body and you will therefore experience the greatest benefit by choosing a crystal to ease and complement your current frame of mind. Luckily there is a vast choice of crystals suitable for meditations. The question is: how to choose the one, which helps you most at this particular moment!

The simplest way to choose your crystal is intuitively. You may find it difficult to believe, but each of us, deep down, has an innate knowledge of our personal needs, physically as well as emotionally. It is a fact that many of us do not trust our own judgement in believing that our choice of crystals is indeed the right one. This is actually quite common. Why not try the following simple exercise the next time? Relax and hold the chosen crystal in your hands for a couple of minutes, close your eyes and sense how it affects you. In most cases you will soon become aware of an energy flowing through your body.

Observe the effect of this energy and if this feels comfortable it is the Right One for you at this moment. Try it and trust yourself. Should you, after you have held the crystal for a few minutes, still have doubts, check it with your pendulum by asking "Is this the best crystal for my meditation at this time"? You may be pleasantly surprised when you receive an affirmative answer.

Having chosen your meditation crystal intuitively a couple of times, and your choice was confirmed to be 'just right', you will find that choosing the crystal you need becomes easier and easier. Your sensitivity to energies of specific crystals will develop fast and, before long, you will be able to choose the most suitable crystal without a second thought.

An alternative is to choose your meditation crystal by the 'Mental Method'. To do this you have to be aware of your needs and also 'know' your crystals. This means you should have a good knowledge of the energies of individual crystals, enabling you to choose the one which can help your emotional needs, or state of mind, to balance your energies. To give an example: you would not choose a crystal which is known to stimulate your mind, or increase your blood pressure when you intend to meditate and need energies which create a calming effect.

To help you along you will find below a list of recommended meditation crystals from which you can choose for your specific circumstances:

Recommended Meditation Crystals

Amethyst	- balancing, aids spiritual connection
Angelite	- warm and relaxing
Blue Lace Agate	- gently clearing
Celestite	- connects us with the Angelic Kingdom
Citrine	- emotionally uplifting
Moss Agate	- clearing, and relaxing
Pink Coral	- gently energising
Rosequartz	- very gentle, surrounds you in a lovely fluffy pink cloud
Moonstone	- emotionally comforting
Larimar	- healing and totally relaxing
Lavender	- gently balancing

At this point it is also important to mention that the foregoing list of crystals should only be looked upon as a guideline, bearing in mind that each person and each crystal has its own unique energy and consequently interaction between each person and each crystal is one of a kind. If at all possible, use crystals in sphere form for maximum effect. Alternatively go for the humble and affordable tumblestones. The reason for this is that the energies in these smooth forms radiate a balanced energy. This is not always the case when 'rough' or 'natural' crystals are used, however beautiful they may be.

How long and often should I meditate?

The duration of a meditation is entirely up to you. It may be an hour, half an hour. 20 minutes or as short as 5 minutes. If you have a very busy life even a short meditation will help to bring you peace and relaxation. If you have the time to yourself you may enjoy a meditation of longer duration.

Another often asked question is: *"How often should I meditate?"* This is entirely your personal choice. Daily would be great, but not many of us can find the time for this in our busy lives, although most of us can find 5 minutes or so to 'sandwich' in a short meditation daily. Also remember that a walk in the woods with your dog and a crystal in your pocket can be a meditation. The rewards of peace and equilibrium gained are well worth the effort!

If you are seriously interested to pursue this practice, you can always join a meditation group. Most of these are held once a week or fortnightly and it is often easier for a beginner to start with, since most of these meditations are guided and therefore easier.

POINTS TO BEAR IN MIND WHEN MEDITATING

In order to remain reasonably grounded during your meditation, it is important to take your shoes off so that the energies of your feet connect to the earth's energies. As the soles of shoes are usually composed of an artificial substance, it impedes energy flow. The direct connection, via the many energy channels in your body and the soles of your feet, with Mother Earth, is very important during meditation. It allows an energy exchange to take place between the spiritual, cosmic energy (entering your Crown Chakra) and the earth's energy (your feet connecting with Mother Earth). This not only benefits your body, but also has a far vaster valuable impact. You are an active medium, creating an energy bridge between heaven and earth, which is beneficial on a large scale. It is great to know that besides remaining 'grounded' we act as transmitters and are able to infuse our needy Mother Earth with high spiritual vibrations.

If you are of a super sensitive nature and know that it is difficult for you to remain, 'in your body' during meditation, I suggest that you place a grounding stone between your feet. Your choice again, is very personal. Normally Red Jasper, Black Tourmaline, or a Hematite will do an admirable job. This will not adversely affect your meditation, but helps to keep you grounded, especially if you are doing a meditation by yourself. My experience over many years, training hundreds of students, have taught me that some people may well be tempted to 'leave' their body and stay 'up there', but this is not the aim of meditation, tempting though it may appear at times!

CRYSTAL MEDITATION

- *Choose an appropriate crystal to hold in your hands*
- *Choose a calm and peaceful environment*
- *Light a candle and if possible an incense stick*
- *Keep both feet on the ground (no shoes!) and remove your watch*
- *Protect yourself by mentally placing a bubble of light around you*

- *If you have a religious belief, ask for help and protection during your meditation of your Guardian Angel, or other High Beings you feel connected to.*
- *Seat yourself in a comfortable position in a chair and keep your spine straight*
- *Try and let go of all tensions and completely relax your body*
- *Take a couple of slow deep abdominal breaths, releasing any remaining tensions on the outbreath*
- *Quieten your mind as much as possible*
- *Hold your chosen crystal loosely in the palm of your left hand which is relaxed in your lap*
- *Loosely cup your right hand over the left hand which is holding the crystal*
- *Become aware of the energy flow of the crystal, gently flooding your entire body; observe what you are experiencing*
- *Enjoy the chosen (calming, energising or, balancing) energy supplied by the crystal, while remaining completely relaxed for as long as you feel comfortable*
- *When you are ready to return to your everyday life, gently and slowly wiggle your toes and move your fingers and hands; take a couple of deep breaths and open your eyes. You may feel you want to gently stretch your arms and move your feet (please do so!)*
- *Become aware of the earth energies through your feet and 'connect' with the earth so that you may be properly grounded*
- *Give thanks to the Angelic Kingdom (and/or others who have assisted you and given their energy) and to the Crystal(s) who generously shared its/their energy with you*
- *Finally protect your seven main chakras by mentally placing the ancient sign of a cross of light within a circle of light upon each one and place yourself in a protective bubble of light, so that you are able to 'safely' return to the' everyday world'.*

AFTER YOUR MEDITATION

Although having discussed this subject earlier in this book, the importance of 'being grounded' cannot be over-emphasised. 'Grounding' means that your energies have to 'come down' to be in tandem with earth vibrations. When meditating we usually find ourselves in an Alpha state; our bodies relax to a high degree and the heart rate slows down, which affects (and benefits) our entire system. After meditation a little time is needed to ensure your body's system is functioning again in keeping with the earth's vibration. In other words: you should be well grounded.

On the odd occasion it may happen that, after a deep meditation, a person may experience a floating or light headed feeling; as though you are not quite in your body. Should this ever be the case, get hold of as large a grounding crystal you have and hold it in your hands, or put it in between your feet, or both! A large Red Jasper tumblestone is a good (and cheap) investment to have handy, should this occur, or a Hematite or Black Tourmaline will do equally well. It also helps to visualise your feet growing roots into the earth. Remember that energy follows thought and this is a very sound and easy way of coming Down To Earth quickly!

The other important part of protection refers to our chakras. These centres are very sensitive. They are constantly taking fresh energy into the body from the environment as well as releasing used energy. When, during meditation, we are completely relaxed, our chakras are wide open to receive the beneficial energy surrounding us. In our everyday world, the energies may not be as pure and we need to protect these sensitive centres. When we visualise a Cross of Light in a circle of Light on the seven main chakras at the end of our meditation, we create this protection. If we should not be sufficiently protected and grounded, we are vulnerable to 'picking up' energies which are not necessary beneficial!

Before finishing this chapter, I would like to side step for a moment. I feel it is important to explain a common misunderstanding. Many people talk about 'closing' one's chakras after a meditation.... Now hold on for a moment! Think about the basic function of our chakras, these important energy centres! To put their functions simple; imagine 'fresh' energy being taken into these centres and 'old used' energy being expelled. Now envision your chakras being closed....! This would put a stop to an energy flow, which is vital to the health and well-being of our body and entire energy system.... For this very reason we 'protect' our chakras in the time honoured spiritual manner with a Cross of Light in a Circle of Light, allowing the energy flow to continue unimpeded, but protected from harm.

To give you an example I would like to relate an experiment told to me and which is purported to have been carried out some decades ago: A leaden shield was placed over the chakras of one brave (or stupid!) volunteer and it only took a few minutes before the poor fellow passed out, looking as white as chalk! The scientists conducting the experiment hastily removed the shields, but it took quite a while for this courageous volunteer to return to normal, and be his old self again.

Having completed your meditation you should now feel good and enjoy a sense of peace and well-being. At this stage it is time to pay some attention to the crystal(s), which so kindly provided you with energy. Check, either by personal sensing, or with your pendulum, whether your crystals need to be cleansed. If you have used any of the crystals mentioned on the foregoing list, they will in most cases be happy to be cleansed by holding them for a few minutes under a running tap of alternating cold and warm water, but if you have used a porous crystal, cleanse it by holding it in incense. On the odd occasion, perhaps when you were very needy, the crystal may need a 'proper' cleanse, such as water with Crab Apple.

Don't be surprised if you find that you need to use this self same crystal for several days, or even weeks, in your meditation. It means that a personal energy adjustment is 'in progress'. This is great! Your particular crystal will assist in bringing about the necessary change or balance in your personal energy system in a gentle and positive way. Again, go by what you feel and learn to trust your intuition!

SUMMARY

Now that you are familiar with the benefits of meditating with your chosen crystals, you may well decide that it is worth the effort to get into a daily meditation routine – however short it may be. We all have busy lives, but you might be able to snatch 5, or perhaps even 10 minutes out of a day? I promise you will enjoy the benefits. Not only will you be rewarded emotionally by feeling calm and able to deal with the challenges of the day, but you will also accelerate your spiritual transformation, which is taking place in this important time of world changes. Crystals have a role to play and by meditating with them we accelerate and facilitate the adjustments our bodies are making, while at the same time assisting in the transformation of the Crystal Kingdom.

****

FIRST AID WITH CRYSTALS

When people tell you that crystals will do 'this' or 'that', do not always believe this as it is not necessarily the case. To give a simple example; your friend may have a pain in her arm and tells you she is greatly helped by rubbing Amethyst on it. If she feels this, great! Although one particular crystal may help one person for a certain condition, this does not necessarily apply to the population at large. Because each of us is so unique (and so are our energies), our reaction to crystal energies may vary considerable. To achieve the maximum healing potential, I strongly believe that choosing the appropriate crystals for certain conditions should only be undertaken by a qualified crystal therapist who has the knowledge and sensitivity to know what is needed.

Nevertheless, there are several time-proven simple techniques with certain crystals, which you can safely apply and which can help to ease every day life. In this chapter you will find a variety of uses, which are both safe and supportive. By the way, when practising personal crystal based exercises, it is sensible to take off your watch as this may impede the energy flow and might well harm your quartz watch (I lost a few watches in my 'early' crystal days before it dawned on me that the energy flow was too much for my watch!).

Clear Quartz Generators for Clearing and Energising

This is a simple way of balancing and re-energising yourself after a hectic day. It can be practised at any time. All you need is a comfortable chair to sit in. You can even do it while watching TV although you benefit more if you relax. You would need two smallish clear quartz generators, approximately 2 inches (5 cm) long. (A Quartz Generator is a point broken off from a cluster and is easily available in various sizes.)

Seat yourself in a comfortable chair; take off your shoes and place both feet on the ground. Take one of the quartz generators and hold it loosely in the palm of your left hand, pointing towards your arm, while the other generator should be placed in the palm of your right hand, pointing towards your fingertips. Relax totally and close your eyes. Breathe evenly and slowly and be aware only of the two crystals held in your hands. Shortly you will become aware of energy going up your left arm and slowly moving through your body, down to the fingertips of your right hand. Stay with this until you feel the energy flowing through your entire body.

On the odd occasion you may feel a slight discomfort temporarily, somewhere in a muscle of your body. This mostly happens in your arm or shoulder. Please do not worry, this will disappear very quickly. The reason for this is that the crystal in your left hand is producing an energy, which travels upwards in your arm and has encountered an energy blockage. It therefore 'pushes' against this blockage in an effort to clear the path and this causes the temporary discomfort. However, once the energy flow has been restored and the energy continues on its way, the discomfort will disappear.

Having restored the energy throughout your body in this way, you will feel a definite benefit from this exercise; you will feel clearer, brighter and energised. Believe me, it is a great 'Pick-me-up' after a demanding or tiring day.

ROSEQUARTZ FOR UPSETS

It is widely acknowledged that Rosequartz is a lovely, gentle Crystal. It spreads comfort, warmth and healing and is available in many forms, from rough pieces to the most exquisite shapes. There is no need to spend a fortune on a piece of Rosequartz (unless you want to!). In addition to the humble tumblestone, it is easily available in the shape of a heart, a small sphere or any other shape. However, if you intend to use it for healing, go for a smooth form. The advantage is that it will distribute the energy more evenly.

Rosequartz is a safe and wonderful crystal to simply hold when you are upset or overwrought. A simple and effective way to benefit would be to take either a single Rosequartz in your left hand or, better still, place a Rosequartz in each hand (tumblestones are ideal). Sit and relax - as much as is physically possible - and breathe slowly and regularly. Feel the Rosequartz in your hands and imagine you are absorbing its lovely calming energies. Soon you will feel a lovely warm glow flooding your body and enveloping you in a gentle pink cloud. Stay in this for at least 15 minutes and you will feel a different person.

This exercise can be done as often as needed.

AMBER TO ASSIST WITH COLD RELIEF

Although Amber does, strictly speaking, not belong to the Crystal Kingdom, it has been accepted by most crystal healers because of its valuable healing potential. Amber is solidified tree resin from ancient trees. It has been in the earth for millions of years and solidified into the beautiful brown to gold looking Amber we know and admire today. It is highly sought after and you probably know it best set in jewellery.

True clear Amber is quite costly. This is probably the reason why there is a lot of imitation (plastic) 'amber' on the market and which is often hard to distinguish from the real thing! Amber comes in several shades; from gold to brown and can sometimes be slightly milky. Of late there has even been some lovely clear green Amber on the market, but because of its rarity the price is higher than the more easily available yellow/brown Larger pieces often have inclusions of insects, caught in the syrupy resin as it dripped down a tree all those millions of years ago. This is much sought after by scientists and fetches high prices.

Amber was highly valued by our ancestors and even has a mystical history woven around it. Devotees hold regular international 'Amber Events'. These often take place in areas such as the Balkans and Dominican Republic, both areas where large amounts of amber have been found.

As such Amber is not strictly a crystal, but due to its special energetic properties it is a valuable therapeutic tool, used by crystal therapists all over the world. It has the reputation of being able to help cold or 'flu sufferers and I can personally vouch this be the case. At the first sign of a cold, get out your Amber necklace and wear it day and night. This will often help to stave off a cold or lessen its unpleasant effects. I strongly advise you that, if your purse stretches to an Amber necklace, it is well worth the investment.

Amber is relatively easy to locate. There are many traders who specialise in Amber and these are usually the best sources. You will find them mainly on health and fitness exhibitions. These people truly know their amber and you can usually rely on them to sell the genuine article. However, if in doubt, take your pendulum with you. Now that you are able to use this valuable instrument it is good to use it in cases like this!

AMETHYST FOR INSOMNIA

Having a good night's sleep is bliss! As long as we enjoy this we take it for granted, until circumstances or somebody upset us. Suddenly we find that sleep does not come easily any more.

Instead of relaxing when we go to bed we fret and worry and somehow sleep escapes us. Our mind is occupied with internal dialogues of how to solve this problem, or how to come to terms with, or deal with this new state of affairs. Before we realise what is happening we tumble into this undesirable pattern called 'insomnia'. Yet, the harder we try to relax and sleep, the more it continues to evade us...

Having suffered many sleepless nights, you become irritable and are no longer your relaxing, loveable self! You realise that you need your sleep and get more and more anxious about this while your original problem is nowhere near a solution. Anything for a good night's sleep! But hold on, before you rush off to your GP for a prescription of sleeping pills, why not give Amethyst a try! Amethyst has been renowned over the ages to relax mind and body and induce sleep. All you need is a simple Amethyst tumble stone. Program it for a fitful relaxing sleep as set out in chapter on " Programming Crystals" and either place it under your pillow, or hold it in your left hand. Simply concentrate on your breathing and be aware of the calming energy of the Amethyst crystal... It is definitely worth a try!

Enjoy a good night's sleep and have sweet dreams!

BLACK TOURMALINE AND YOUR COMPUTER

You may recall that this subject is discussed in detail in the chapter on Protection, however I find it such an important subject that I want to briefly mention it again since it is now scientifically acknowledged that spending a lot of time working on your computer may have a detrimental affect on us. If you are one of those people affected by electronic equipment, you would do well to invest in half a dozen of these important crystals and place them in front of the electronic apparatus in your home as protection.

SODALITE - THE PERSONAL PROTECTOR

The benefits of this amazing crystal have already been discussed in detail in the earlier chapter on Protection, but because of its immense importance, I cannot help but remind my readers of the wonderful protection and help Sodalite has to offer. If you are uncomfortable in your working environment, do give it a try and carry a piece of Sodalite in your pocket and experience the difference for yourself.

CITRINE - FOR JOY

The most loved crystal in our courses is Citrine. Not only because it is a very important healing tool in the Crystal Therapist's kit, but because it is affectionally known as 'The Happy Crystal'. Whenever we have been sensing Citrine in class, everybody gets the giggles and the general atmosphere is a jolly one!

Citrine has the most amazing healing properties in the hands of a qualified crystal healer but it can also be of great help on days when we feel 'down in the dumps'. My friends know that, when they see me wearing my Citrine necklace, I need some help seeing the sunny side of life!

For us girls, the best you can do is treating yourself to a Citrine chip necklace. These are relatively inexpensive and very quickly fill your entire aura with this nice and bright energy. As to the fellows, my best suggestion to you is to carry a couple of nice crystal tumblestones in your pocket. Just one piece of advice: Citrine needs a lot of cleansing if you want to get the best out of it. So cleanse it daily after wearing it.

You may also be interested to know that, in times gone by, Citrine was greatly valued by all kinds of merchants, who carried it in their cash containers. They were convinced that with a piece of this golden looking crystal in their purse or moneybag, the cash would keep flowing in! Whether it worked or not, I have not been able to find out but, just in case, why not try it? Believing in it goes a long way!

Restoring Jaded Plants to Life

We have all been away on holiday, thoroughly enjoying ourselves, and returning to a home with drooping plants, somehow taking the edge of your happy holiday.... During your absence your offspring, or a kind neighbour who took the task upon her to care for your plants, either forgot to water them, or overdid it. Consequently, your precious plants are either dried up or drowned (if my experience is anything to go by!). In an effort to salvage them, you waste no time and put the 'dried-up' plants in a bowl of water, while you allow the too generously watered plants to dry out and hope for the best!

So far, it may not have occurred to you, but do you realise that crystals can be a great help in restoring life to this poor jaded foliage? The best thing you can do in these cases, once you have watered, or dried out your pots with greenery, is to surround them with crystals, 'feeding' them crystalline energy. Simply follow the example given in the illustration below, making sure you direct the points of the four Quartz Crystals towards the plant. You should leave the crystals surrounding your 'victims' until they have fully recovered and you will be surprised how quickly this can happen with the help from your crystals.

Assisting Plant Growth

If you are a keen gardener, or someone who loves plants and takes cuttings, crystals can also direct their energy to accelerate growth. The pattern to follow is similar to the foregoing.

If you want to verify this for yourself take two similar cuttings. Do this in the same way you would normally do it, but surround one newly potted cutting with four quartz crystals, pointing towards the pot; you leave the second one without crystals. Now watch how the cutting surrounded by the four Quartz Crystals 'takes off'. The difference may astonish you.

ENERGISING YOUR GARDEN

You don't have to be a keen gardener wanting to see your garden in full bloom, similar to those idyllic pictures in garden magazines. One way to achieve this is with the help of Quartz Crystals. In this way you can bring energy into your garden and watch as your flowers and veggies thrive! It was a North American Indian friend who taught me an ancient manner of fertilising one's entire garden, which he said, had been practised by his people as long as he could remember. I have personally tried it and been awarded with an abundance of flowers and fruit crop every year.

In a similar way as used above, to regenerate individual plants, we once again call upon the assistance of our four Quartz Crystals. This time the intention is to create a much larger grid to encompass our entire garden. The principle is the same as in the foregoing methods, but the crystals used should be larger. I suggest that the four Quartz crystals should be approximately 3 to 3½ inches (8 – 10 cm) long. In addition to these four we need one additional crystal. This one should be a large Quartz Generator of 4 – 4½ inches (10 – 12 cm) long and about 1 – 1½ inches (3 – 4 cm) in diameter.

METHOD

Place the four smaller generators on the four corners of the garden, with their points facing towards the centre. Place the large Quartz Crystal as near as possible in the exact centre of your garden in the ground upright. The effect will be that energy is drawn into the garden via the corner crystals. As you already know from a previous chapter, energy is drawn into a crystal at the blunt end and comes out at its point, focussed, purified and amplified, thus directing its pure wholesome energy into your garden and directing it to the centre where your large Quartz Generator is standing upright. This crystal will receive the already amplified energy from the four directions and the purifying/energising principle repeats itself and the energies are amplified further. As the apex of this crystal is pointing upwards, the result is that the energy is going up and in this way act likes an energy fountain, 'spraying' the entire garden with its nourishing, energies.

To help you make the most of this exercise, I suggest that, before placing your crystals in the garden, you dedicate them to fertilisation and nourishment of your plants and flowers. Furthermore, it would be a lovely gesture that, before you 'place and plant' your crystals, you carry out a little ceremony to call in the assistance of the fairies and other little inhabitants in your garden. They not only love to help, but have a great affinity with the crystal kingdom. They will appreciate what you are doing and, when asked, will be delighted to help. This ceremony need be very simple. Sit down somewhere in your garden (the lawn if you have one would be a perfect place) and tune into nature and those many unseen little workers. Tell them how much you appreciate what they have been, and are, doing for your garden. Let them know that you are going to place these five very especially dedicated crystals in their space with an energy they will enjoy, and how much you would appreciate their cooperation in making it a specially nice garden.

The little people will really be delighted and, besides having a healthy and beautiful garden you will find that it becomes a haven of peace for all to enjoy.

Clearing a Room from Negativity

Have you ever entered a hotel room and 'felt' that its energies were, to put it simply 'not nice'? Due to a job I had at the time, I spent up to three months a year travelling abroad, and had no option but to spend many a night in hotel rooms. This accommodation had often been pre-booked for me by kind clients, so I had little choice in the matter!

As hotel rooms are used by many people, it is inevitable that some energy from previous occupiers are left and, although physical cleansing was in most cases meticulous, it was inevitable that a lot remained on an energetic level. Many of these travellers would be on business far away from home and often anxious to conclude a sale, which might, or might not, work out. They also might have other worries on their minds, creating a tense and unhappy atmosphere. Luckily for them, most of the newly arrived guests would be blissfully unaware whether energies were good or, let's say, 'unpleasant'. Unlucky though for people with more than average sensitivity, i.e. those of us aware of these offensive remainders from previous visitors.

Whenever it was my unfortunate fate to land in an energetically 'polluted' hotel room, I would set to work by bringing in the light and calling for help from the great Archangel Michael. However in most cases, after what had been a tough day, I would arrive in my room physically and mentally exhausted and this cleansing took time and effort. On the odd occasion when I was too tired, or forgot, I would have a disturbing night.

It was not until several years later, when I was on a 'crystal' holiday in Arkansas with my friend Louise visiting crystal mines, that a solution was presented. Like me, Louise is equally enthralled with crystals and has a close connection with the Crystal Kingdom. One night we 'ended up' in a doubtful little guesthouse. Previous visitors, with negative energies, had clearly visited the one and only remaining room available, which was allocated to us, and left a legacy of not-so-nice residue behind! No problem said Louise, and produced her 'travel kit', which consisted of a pretty little box containing one medium size piece of Selenite, one single Quartz Generator, one Rosequartz sphere and one Smokey Quartz sphere. She laid them out in the pattern set out and within an hour the entire room was clear and felt good. This was a fabulous solution! Had I but known of this ten or so years ago and life would have been a lot more comfortable! Alas, crystals were not the centre of my life in those days. However, I did not waste any time and immediately created my own 'crystal travel kit', which was (and still is) in a small wooden box in my ever ready-to-travel beauty case. Since then, it has travelled around the globe more than once, and cleared many a room en route. I truly consider this little kit one of the most indispensable companions whenever I travel, or even go somewhere just for the weekend. Experience has taught me that you never know when you need it!

ROOM CLEARANCE LAY-OUT

Quartz Crystal

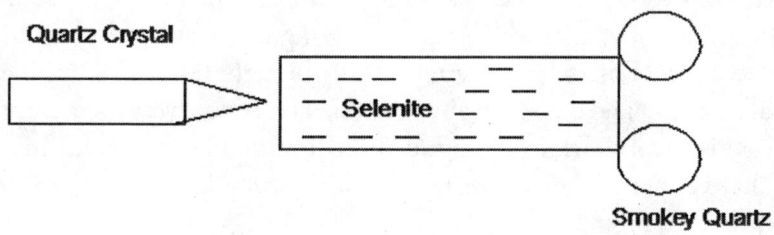

Rosequartz

Selenite

Smokey Quartz

Practical Points

The quartz generator need be no longer than 4 cm (or 1¾ inches)
The Selenite can be anything from 5 to 6 cm (or 2 inches)
The Rosequartz and Smokey Quartz spheres should be approximately 2 cm (or ¾ inch) in diameter, but may also be substituted with similar size tumblestones.

Whenever you want to clear a room, set out the above pattern as soon as you arrive. You can even put it unobtrusively in a draw if you do not want it to be seen by curious hotel staff. It will still work. You can count on it that in an hour's time the energy in the most intolerant room will be clear and pleasant. It may not be necessary but I usually leave this clearing pattern until I depart the next day, leaving the room clearer and fresher than it had probably been for a long time!

It is important to remember that the Quartz generator, the Rosequartz and the Smokey Quartz need cleansing after having worked so hard. Selenite has a very high energy and does not need cleansing.

Energising Water

With today's general pollution, the water that we receive through our taps is no longer what it used to be… (Good old days!) From necessity the Water Companies add all kinds of chemicals to it to make it safe for us to drink. Add to this environmental contamination and is it a wonder that we all need purifying filters or bottled water? The necessity of filtering our water is really brought home after having installed a filter and on putting in a new filter one once every six months or so. It is a real shock to see so much accumulated gunge, which may well have the effect of another trip to the supermarket to top up your bottled water supply.

Although most bacteria have been killed through these processes and harmful substances have been removed by our filtering; it still means that the water, which originally comes out of our taps, has no energy whatsoever. If you find this hard to believe, why don't you find this out for yourself? You can do this with the help of your pendulum. I presume that, after reading the earlier chapter about dowsing, you have practised working with this invaluable tool! You now have a chance to practise by finding out the energy of water; in a similar way you used your pendulum to find out the energy of your crystals. By holding your pendulum over a glass of water fresh from the tap and asking it "Does this water have energy?", you will sadly discover that the above information is true.

To the rescue comes the simple but very powerful Quartz Crystal again! You have already seen the positive difference crystals can make to our environment and us and they are not letting us down here either! All you need are a few little Quartz Crystals to bring life back into our drinking water.

To begin with purchase three small Quartz crystals (rough or tumblestones) of approximately 1 inch (3 cm) diameter. If you have a filtering system or are straining your water in one of the many commercial filters, your water is already purified and all that remains is to energise the water. This is very simple; place the three small Quartz Crystals at the bottom of a large jug and fill it with water, leaving them four to five hours undisturbed (overnight is a good idea). On rising the next morning treat yourself to a glass of this lovely 'crystal' water. You will be surprised how good it tastes; so much nicer and clearer! Get your pendulum out to check its energy and you will find that your crystal water is highly energised. It is ideal to drink, but also great for making your teas and coffees as well as in cooking. Simply by using this water you bring fresh energy into your body and (particularly if you drink the recommended 8 glasses a day) it should enhance your energy level.

You will be pleased to know that the four to five hours of soaking the crystals need not be repeated. To keep this process going the secret is to never completely empty your jug, but always leave sufficient water to keep the crystals covered. Then simply fill the jug up again and again. In this way you will have energised crystal water for the next three months. After that period, your little crystals need a rest. Remove the crystals from the jug and replace them with fresh ones. Place the used ones in the sun so they can rest and receive energy themselves, ready to assist you again in another three months' time. Since these little fellows are very affordable, I suggest you invest in an additional set. Meantime, repeat the process from scratch with your newly acquired and properly cleansed set and you will enjoy another three months of crystal water. At the end of these months your original little crystals will be ready once more to help you.

Enjoy your very own healthy 'crystal water' and the '8 glasses a day' will no longer be a chore!

****

ANIMAL HEALING

Animals are very sensitive to energies. This is easy to understand when one considers that their survival in nature relies on their being aware of energies. This basic instinct still is present in our domesticated animals. There are numerous stories of both cats and dogs having advanced knowledge that their owner, or a family member loved by the pet, is due to arrive home shortly. They are excited, look out of the window or wait behind the door and, of course, know the sound of their owner's car engine. With my own poodle, I merely need to think "walkies time" and he appears from nowhere, barking excitedly at the thought of his outing, jumping up like a Jack-in-the-box!

My students have told me stories of their animals who love to lie under their couch, or be near them, while treatment was in progress. Frequently cats jump on the lap of the person receiving healing and in this way ensure they got a share of the healing energies. There are times when clients do not necessarily appreciate this.

Many years back I was involved in moving zoo animals all over the globe. Whenever physically possible I would travel with them in transport planes, sitting along the crates on a bale of hay. Being put into a crate for the duration of the journey is very traumatic for animals, but the zoos I worked with were very responsible and their staff always took great care to ensure that these moves would take place with as little upset to the animals as possible. Feeding them in their crates weeks before the transport took place often minimised their stress and ensured the animal in question would accept this as 'home'. Zebras are notoriously nervous and whenever the animals of this species had to be moved, I made sure to be there to accompany them. I spent many an hour before official loading onto the aircraft took place sitting next to their crates in the big draughty hangers, as transport planes seemed to be forever subject to unexpected delays. In order to calm them down I would talk to them, all the while holding an appropriate crystal and sending healing to the nervous animals. This helped to quieten them considerably. The guys working at Heathrow at the time got to know me well and were amused. Eventually I became known as 'the Zebra Woman'.

Bijou

I have been fortunate to live with dogs all my life, and have come across many experiences of doggie-crystal-awareness. I had a beautiful white miniature poodle called Bijou. He loved crystals more than any dog I have known before or since. We used to have a weekly meditation group in my house and I would always choose a specific crystal to place in the centre of the circle on the floor. One of my special crystals is a beautiful Amethyst generator about eight inches tall. This particular crystal was frequently placed in the centre of the circle during our meditation.

It was almost as though Bijou knew that it was this particular crystal's 'turn' to proudly stand in the middle and he would be waiting. To the amusement of the group he would almost stand to attention! An immaculate pretty white cloth would be put down and the moment the Amethyst touched the ground, Bijou would drape himself around it, claiming the crystal as his.

While the crystals we used during our meditations would vary, he never bothered about others. It was just this particular Amethyst. His taste in crystals was impeccable. Naturally, we gave him an Amethyst pendant, which we fixed onto his collar and, apart from a regular cleanse; he wore it until he departed for heavenly regions.

In canine terms, Bijou was a very advanced spiritual poodle. Whenever I gave healing to someone, he would wriggle his way between my patient and myself. Once he had achieved this he would stretch out comfortably with a satisfied sigh, often making it difficult on a practical level to get around my patient. When giving treatments on the couch, he would love to lie below it and stayed there very quietly without moving. All he wanted to do was to soak up the crystal healing energies.

At one time Bijou suffered from a kidney infection and was given an injection by the vet with instructions to bring him back in a week's time. While trying to figure out which crystal might help him, he surprised us by making an amazing recovery and, consequently, there was no point in a follow-up visit to the vet. It was not until a couple of weeks later when I found he had somehow helped himself to one of my largish Prehnite tumblestones and buried it in his basket under his blanket... Prehnite has been known to have a healing effect on kidneys. It clearly had done Bijou a world of good and he never suffered a recurrence. Needless to say I left the Prehnite where it was, in his basket, apart from the occasional cleanse. Like food, most animals know what is and what is not good for them.

How You Can Help Your Animals With Crystals

As mentioned earlier, domestic animals are very sensitive to energies, whether they are environmental, human or crystal. As crystal lovers we have a wonderful opportunity to help our four-footed companions. This can be done in a very simple way by attaching a suitable crystal to the animal's collar. An Amethyst, for instance, is a very good balancer if your dog tends to be hyperactive or nervous. Try to use crystals that are familiar to you. In other words, don't go over the top by giving your dog or cat an exotic new crystal you have just discovered on your last visit to the Crystal Exhibition, unless you are familiar with its energies.

If you are by now handy in using the pendulum, I suggest you check to ascertain whether the crystal you have chosen is right for your pet at the time of need. Should you choose incorrectly, don't worry, you will find out soon enough. Your canine or feline friends have ways and means to let you know. They are very inventive as well as sensitive. Not long after you supply them with your choice of a particular 'healing' crystal you will wonder where it has gone. How could he/she possibly have lost a crystal you fastened so securely to his or her collar? It clearly was not the 'right' crystal for your canine or feline friend.

Giving your pet 'crystal water' is another way of helping to keep him/her energised and balanced. The recipe is described in the 'First Aid with Crystals' chapter and is equally beneficial for humans and pets.

Just a note of warning: Please do not put crystals in your pet's water bowl as he/she might accidentally swallow them. This actually happened to a friend of mine who acted with the best intentions. She wondered where the tumblestones went until her dog became ill and had to be operated on to remove what the vet irreverently called 'those d….. stones' from his stomach!

****

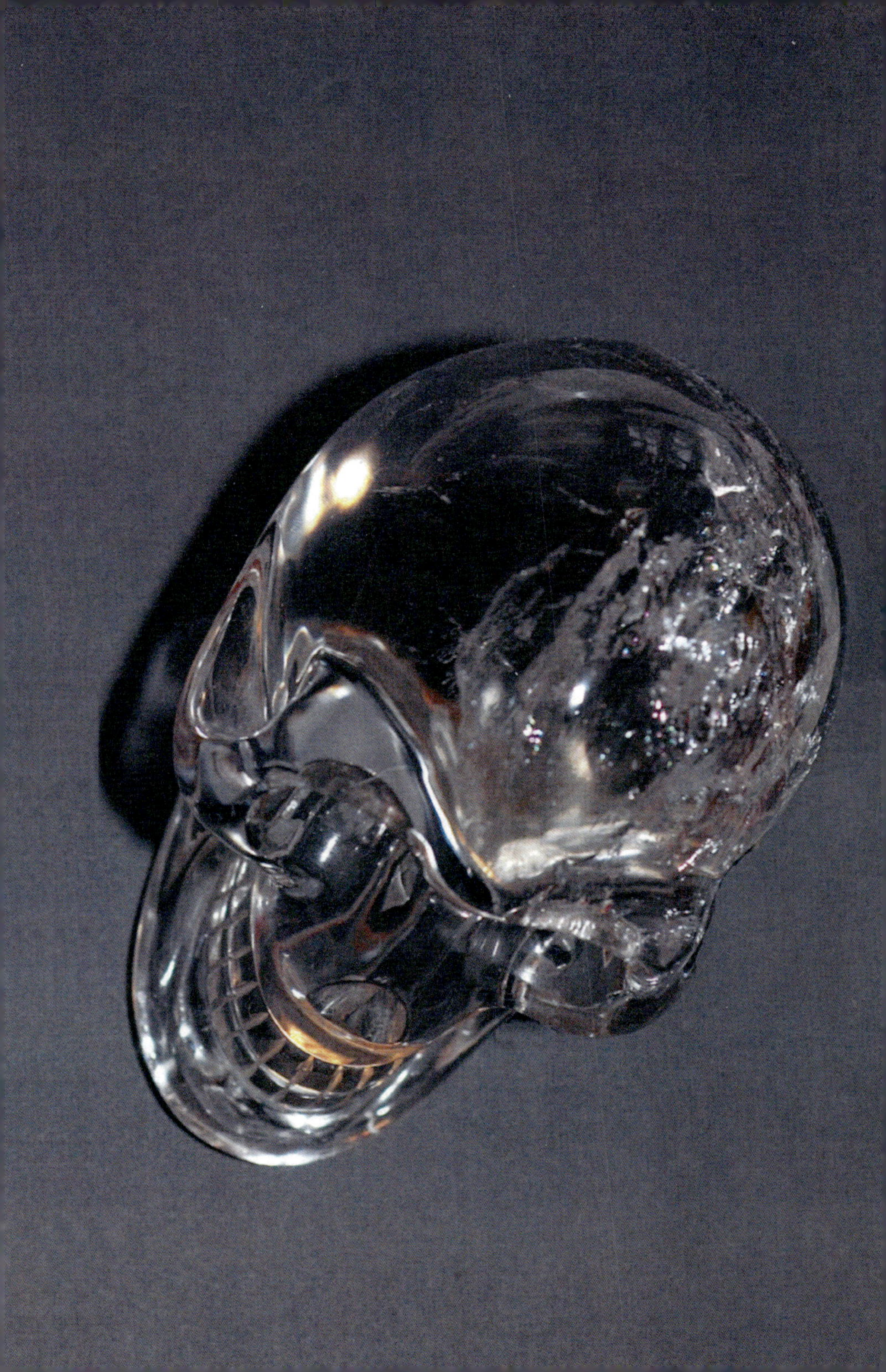

CRYSTAL SKULL

THE SECRET MISSION OF CRYSTALS

THE CRYSTAL'S SOUL JOURNEY

When thinking about 'crystal healing' you may conjure up a mental picture of the healing effect crystals have on our physical bodies. However, strange as it may sound, few of us realise that we can assist in 'healing' crystals themselves or support them on their own specific 'soul's journey'.

This was brought home to me very clearly some years ago when it was my fortune to acquire a very special crystal with whom I can communicate. He is a very old and wise being. You might call him a 'crystal philosopher'! Getting in touch with him in meditation, I asked to be given information on the true purpose of Crystal Life on Earth. The following reply was received:

The Crystals' Life Purpose is:
- To be of service in a different dimension
- To touch people and make them aware of their divine origin
- To heal and balance people
- To help change human energies
- To alter human perceptions
- To open people up to different dimensions and spiritual awareness
- To discover human needs and supply the required energy where it is needed to effect positive changes.

"Each of us (different crystal species) has a specific energy to offer which fills particular needs in the individual human energy system".

In giving service we (the Crystal Kingdom) evolve.

Obviously, there are many different schools of thought about the 'functions' of crystals, but the overriding opinion is that crystals are here to help us heal on many levels. Naturally, the method of 'how to' differs widely. It is generally thought that all crystals are instant 'healers', that is, you simply put a certain crystal on a painful spot and, presto, it will relieve the pain, or heal a certain illness. This sounds nice and simple and wouldn't that be great! In practice this is not quite in keeping with the Crystal's Philosophy as set out on the foregoing page. The way crystal healing works is much more subtle, as explained elsewhere in this book.

In keeping with the above given message, the Crystal's mission on this planet goes way beyond physical healing. I believe their 'task' is manifold. We continue to learn about this task as we work with crystals with intention and integrity. In keeping with energy changes taking place on a global level, personal energies are also changing, and with it our emotional and physical needs. My belief is that crystals have an important part to play in the overall well-being of the human race at this time. This includes healing for humans on an emotional level as well as curing physical illnesses. Consequently this, in turn, has an influence on our spiritual evolution. An essential part of this includes learning to live in a state of peace and well-being within oneself on every level. To this end crystals are ready to offer their services, but we on our part need to cooperate and consciously open ourselves up to their energy.

My personal belief is that we come into this world provided with what architects would call a 'blue-print'. Thus, there is a road-map for this particular earthly journey; a careful plan prepared before incarnation, which outlines the lessons we have the opportunity to learn in our life. This might be in the form of challenges we come across this lifetime, offering us the opportunity for maximum spiritual progress. Or, it might give us a chance to form deep bonds with certain people. When being 'shown' this plan while still in a celestial environment, we were most likely full of enthusiasm about these wonderful opportunities to make progress. Only when we arrived in our physical body did the 'physical' reality hit us as these opportunities presented themselves!

It is during these physical and emotionally laden periods that we need the strength to overcome, or come to terms with, the challenges that are being offered. When faced with reality, we do our utmost to deal with this particular situation to the best of our ability, and hopefully, having learned yet another lesson, move forward once again and return to 'normal life'. With additional strength gained, we hope to have the emotional muscle to deal with the next bit of 'spiritual growth' when it comes along! Often all too soon!   If you are lucky, you will have good friends or family around who will support you during these challenging times but, not even the best of friends can be there all the time. If you are religious, you may turn to prayer. If you find the challenge unbearable, you may be tempted to indulge in a glass or two of the strong stuff, or even drugs, to kill the physical and/or emotional pain.

Yet, there is other positive help available. Fortunately, a growing number of people are aware of the many complementary energy therapies available to sustain and support them during these periods of trial. Amongst these, crystal healing is perhaps the 'youngest' of these therapies to be accepted since it's resurfacing in the past fifteen or so years, yet it is fast gaining recognition for its effectiveness.

In an emotional and/or physical crisis we can turn to and find specific crystals which can help us cope. The wonderful thing here is that we all know intuitively which crystals to choose. The one we choose will help us cope, give support both spiritually and emotionally, and in addition, it may be able to ease certain physical conditions. Believe it or not, but everyone has the inner knowing to choose the most suitable crystal at any given time. Every one reading this book can benefit from this subtle help. Should you have any doubt please refer to the chapter on "Choosing crystals" and follow the methods outlined. You will soon find that choosing the Right Crystal becomes second nature. The crystals are just waiting for an opportunity to be of service to humankind and they take great delight in doing so.

The Birth of Crystals

Let us take a look at the life of crystals. These beautiful beings have been growing and maturing slowly in the earth for thousands and thousands of years in order to emerge at the right time to take on their specific task, their 'individual life plan'; which is being of service to humankind, either physically, emotionally or spiritually.

The mining of crystals could be compared to a birthing process. Until crystals are taken from the womb of Mother Earth, they are part of a Mother crystal. Being torn away from the Mother vein is a painful process for crystals. Once they leave the womb and are exposed to daylight, they are thoroughly cleansed and truly in need of a rest to recover from the birthing shock.

Anyone with sensitivity who has ever visited crystal mines and been in the company of newly mined crystals will pick up on this. Ideally these crystals should have the opportunity to convalesce from their birth trauma. However, in the commercial world only a few of the people involved in the mining process are aware of the needs of crystals and it is rarely financially viable to give them time to rest. Incredible though it may seem, there are a few mines, which do give their newly mined crystals time to convalesce, and their crystals reflect the care they have received. They look bright and glowing and their energy is high.

Over the years it has been my privilege to give crystal workshops in the United States as well as in European countries. While teaching in the U.S it has become a custom to add a week onto this trip to visit some of the crystal mines in Arkansas. Together with my friend Louise we go on this delightful annual pilgrimage, doing nothing else but visiting a fair number of the quartz crystal mines. We have come to know these places well and enjoy 'doing the round'. All these mines have a great attraction, but there is one small one where we spend most of our time. In this place the crystals are carefully mined, often with the use of wooden tools and once mined, receive the respect and attention previously described. As a result the crystals in their tiny shop are literally radiating. The owner knows us well and is all too happy to welcome appreciative visitors who share his passion for these beautiful treasures.

To us his shop is a true 'Aladdin's cave' and appropriately enough it has a hidden section where the 'Crystal Connoisseurs' are allowed to spend some time with his favourites. These are many and oh so special! By now you may be conjuring up a luxurious place with comfortable chairs catering for these Special Guests and trays displaying these glittering treasures... Not so. In keeping with treasure grottos we find ourselves uncomfortably squatting in what is best described as a large cupboard. Both walls are lined with shelves containing brown boxes full of the most precious of crystals, and sitting cross legged in a narrow galley between, we are allowed to open each and every box and drool! Uncomfortable? Yes! But by golly, spending a day in this Santa's grotto is the best part of the whole trip.

The above story illustrates that there are indeed caring crystal people, although small in number. However, as we do not yet live in a perfect world, we can but hope, if only because of their beauty and financial value, that commercially mined crystals will receive fairer care in years to come. When this happens sufficient time will have elapsed by the time they appear in crystal shops for these crystals to have recuperated from their 'birthing' process.

Their actual recovery time varies considerably. If crystals have been treated with reasonable care they heal quite quickly, but if they have been 'blasted' out of the earth with dynamite it may take several years. I have come across some large crystals which needed a long time to get over their trauma. At my first visit to the crystal mines in Arkansas, I was drawn to a beautiful large Quartz crystal which I simply could not leave behind. After a lengthy plane journey with this newly acquired friend on my lap (and several airport changes) I arrived back home in the U.K. It was only after meditating with this big 'fellow' that I learned he had spent all his energy attracting my attention and needed a lot of tender loving care and rest to recuperate. He chose to live unobtrusively tucked away on a little corner table in my living room for two years until fully recovered. He simply needed to take it easy until his healing was complete and is now enjoying active service.

If crystals are given a chance to recover after being mined and allowed to adjust to their new environment, they generally become aware of their individual 'calling'. They know they are here to give service and generously make their energies available for the many needy purposes of humankind, either in the scientific, technological, or healing arena.

In order to do their best healing work, they need to work jointly with a dedicated man or woman, capable of channelling true unselfish healing energies. If working professionally as a crystal healer, this dedicated healer should have in-depth knowledge and understanding of the crystals' individual energy. He/she should also know how, when and where to direct their natural frequencies to obtain true healing on all levels -- physically, emotionally, mentally and spiritually.

As discussed previously, the very best and effective way to access this healing energy is to sit or lie down, relax and gently hold the crystal in your hands, allowing it to do its healing work. You will be surprised how powerful this can be. For more information on this subject refer to the chapter 'First Aid with Crystals'

Do not fall into the trap thinking that 'more is better' and hold half a dozen or more crystals. It is easy to get carried away when we see these beautiful beings and it is so easy to forget how powerful they are. Just holding a single tumblestone in your hands often can provide a little miracle.

THE SERVICE OF ONE LITTLE CRYSTAL

Crystals often give help to humans in a quiet and unobtrusive way. The following story is an example of how one little crystal played its part and helped in the transformation of the life of one human being.

Many of us are getting used to seeing crystals in the most unexpected places. They have a place of honour in many homes, but today you may find them in offices, garden centres, markets, bookshops, and even in public places. After all, crystals have a job to do and they make themselves known in the market place – wherever that may be. The Crystal Collective 'inspires' certain individuals to put crystals in these places for a reason. It may be their beauty in the first place that attracts people, but do not underestimate their "guise"; their splendour has purpose.

Imagine the window of a crystal shop. The crystals may appear as simple decorations, but don't be fooled, they are hard at work filling their environment with special energies. Some passer-by, in need of a particular vibration for his/her well-being, either physically or emotionally, but unaware of this, may suddenly 'see' a specific little crystal amongst dozens of these beautiful beings on display, even though there are others that may be bigger and more gorgeous. The crystal in question is hard at work beaming out its energy, which is subconsciously received by the needy passer-by. Strong energy is needed to resist the pulling power of this little being and before this passer-by realises what has happened, he or she enters the shop and leaves with this beautiful little treasure tucked deep in purse or pocket, all the while totally unaware of the changes this may bring into his or her life.

At first, our shopper cannot stop looking at it and admiring this little treasure. The new owner may carry this crystal on his or her person or perhaps will place it near the bed or under the pillow at night. All the while the crystal is tenderly 'doing its job', that is, sending out the right frequencies needed by this person. After a while, gentle changes take place in our crystal shopper. Then one day, the conversation at work turns to 'crystals' and, surprise, surprise, this person learns that his or her friend or colleague also has some crystals and is eager to exchange experiences. This is the moment when the (crystal) ball really starts rolling! They have a common interest and may jointly decide to visit the crystal shop nearby where the process repeats itself, but now the buyers are more open to crystal energies. They may choose some more crystals. They may pick up a leaflet about a crystal workshop and there we are -- a gentle transformation has begun. The little crystal has done its job. It has given service and from now on positive changes will accelerate in the life of our friend.

'SERVICE' OF CRYSTALS

You may be aware why you are in this incarnation at this time and maybe you know of your specific task. Whatever it may be in many cases, it can be expressed in one word: "service". We have a lot more in common with the Crystal Kingdom than our biological resonance.

Service comes in many guises. As a mental exercise let us consider that you, as a caring person, desperately want to help people and make healing your profession. This may be as an Aromatherapist, Reflexologist, or Spiritual Healer. Instead of doing this, however, you find yourself in an office environment because of economic necessity; while all the while you have this strong desire to be 'out there', doing healing and helping people in this way. Even though you follow courses, have your diplomas and feel ready to 'do your bit', you find yourself stale-mate in an administrative job that you hate, in a hectic office where many of your colleagues are trying to cope with the complicated process of living in today's stressful world. Or, you may be a mum with several kids to bring up and somehow there is neither time nor money to do that healing course, which you so much want to do...... Or, your job may be that of a teacher, bus driver or shop keeper. The list is endless but the feelings are the same.

It is easy to forget that being a 'healer' does not necessarily mean 'hands-on' or practising a therapy. Being a good listener to someone in an emotional turmoil can be very, very healing, kissing a sore knee better or being a helpful neighbour is rendering 'service'. Giving a friend a certain crystal in their time of need is 'service'.

In your particular job or environment you have the unique opportunity to reach people in surroundings where no official 'healers' work. The very thought of going to a healer might freak some people out. Yet by simply being there at the Right Time you can listen to somebody's troubles, or give a helping hand as a neighbour, perhaps by giving somebody a little Rosequartz tumblestone to calm and soothe them. 'Healing' can come in many forms, at many times, wherever you are and whatever your task. At this moment you can perform a service to other human beings expressing your uniqueness in the healing spot you find yourself. This might not be quite the way you imagine it should be, but clearly your 'service' is at this moment in a place where only you can do it.

Crystals work in a similar way, as shown in the little tale above. Their true vocation is service. As you have seen from the stories told, these little beings are eager to play their part to help you to help others.

You will have deduced from the Crystal Decree at the start of this chapter, that crystals, like us, have their own evolutionary agenda. Every time they help us, or assist us on behalf of others, they advance their own evolution and in doing so, 'upgrade' their own frequencies, while helping us in our transformation. What a staggering thought that we have a deeply symbiotic relationship with crystals. Crystals are powerful, yet humbling.

****

WHO ARE THE EARTHKEEPERS?

If you have read Katrina Raphaell's books[12,*], you will already know of the existence of the Earthkeepers. Should you not yet be familiar with the concept 'Earthkeepers', allow me to tell you a little about these wonderful Crystal Beings.

Earthkeepers are very large crystals, which can be of any shape or form, but in all cases are Quartz crystals. They may be a huge quartz point, either singly or with one or more points 'sprouting' from the sides, or they may manifest as clusters. Their sizes vary tremendously. There is a 'baby' that lives permanently in the Iraivan temple on the Hawaiian isle of Kaua'i. It is four to five feet high. On the other end of the spectrum there is a gigantic cluster that resides in the Himalayan Mountains.

According to channelled information, there are twelve major Earthkeepers, strategically located within or on the earth. Some work from within the earth, whereas others are happy to do their job on the surface. With the tremendous energy they are capable of emitting, they are extraordinarily powerful.

Besides these twelve major Earthkeepers, there are a large number of minor ones. The major ones are often located in

---

12 *Please refer to bibliography for details of Katrina Raphaell's books.

mountainous areas and are still in the earth, protected from undesirable energies. One of the exceptions is the Earthkeeper in the Hawaiian island of Kaua'i previously mentioned. When I was talking to one of the monks during a visit several years ago, he said that it was actually brought to the island from the U.S. mainland to be at its destination, which is the place where this Earthkeeper is meant to contribute its special energies for the greater good at the right time. It is my understanding that each of the main Earthkeepers has a special guardian, who in most cases has a close connection with a group of highly spiritual people involved in activating them.

Since Earthkeepers, while in the earth, are partially dormant, it is essential that their energies be activated to enable them to project their energies for the highest good of humanity and Mother Earth. This is done by honouring them through meditation, sending them love and wherever physically accessible, perform suitable ceremonies. At this time several of the main Earthkeepers have been either completely or partially activated.

To understand something more about them, we have to go way, way back, in time when these special crystals started life deep within the earth with a special mission. During their growth they accumulated a lot of light energy, while at the same time creating a record of the history of our Mother Earth and life upon her. This was part of their assignment. Theirs was an important task. They were to prepare for a far off future when great changes would take place on the planet and in humanity. At that time, their accumulated light and wisdom would be needed in helping to create Divine Order. That time has arrived now! These special crystal giants are very nearly ready to commence their important task. When all of them are fully activated they will send out their shafts of light and connect to each other to create a light grid of high frequency around our planet. This will give considerable support to aide the positive changes, which take place within the earth and all life upon her.

I owe a lot to Katrina Raphaell who made me aware of the existence of Earthkeepers. I clearly remember reading her book and being filled with a strong urge to see the Kaua'i Earthkeeper, little knowing at the time that this baby Earthkeeper, as well as many of its 'mates', would play an important part in my crystal consciousness.

To my delight this opportunity came sooner than expected. It was in the early nineties when my sister Miep and I were getting ready for a once-in-a-lifetime round-the-world trip; something we had aimed to do for a long time. The first stops were in the United States, so what was easier than making a small detour to Kaua'i? At that time we needed permission to visit the temple and pay homage to this 'baby' Earthkeeper. Having written to the people in charge, this was granted and Miep and I were able to spend a whole day in this place of amazingly high energy.

We flew in to Kaua'i from the big island and were impressed by its beauty. The island was quite small and it took us only one hour to reach our destination. Having rented a car for the day we asked for directions to the little Iraivan temple and were surprised that everyone seemed to be familiar with this temple and the resident Earthkeeper. The temple was set in a beautiful garden. Occasionally, very helpful monks were happy to chat with us and to answer our many questions. The highlight, of course, was entering the temple and seeing the Earthkeeper Crystal for ourselves. She was amazing; as was the energy she exuded! She was surrounded with fresh flowers and adorned with a beautiful silver lingam. A few monks were present in the temple, but one monk was meditating in front of the crystal. At the appointed time, another monk would take his place, after a ceremony of blessings had taken place, which was carried out by the newly arrived monk. This monk would come in and walk, chanting around the crystal, blessing it with incense and adorning it with fresh beautiful tropical flowers. Later we learned that a monk would be meditating there at all times - twenty-four hours a day.

By the time we saw this crystal she was halfway clear. In most cases these crystals, having been in the protective womb of Mother Earth, are covered with a milky frost and appear quite milky inside. However, when activated they begin to clear and eventually become 'crystal clear' - an apt metaphor! This, by the way, is a happening I have witnessed at home with some of my more humble crystals. You, the reader, may well have experienced this with your own crystals. This is a phenomenon which may happen when you meditate regularly with the same quartz crystal or, work with it continually in a healing environment. Many of my students have also experienced this.

However, returning to the story of our Hawaiian Earthkeeper; I was hoping that by now she would be completely clear. Shortly after our visit, access to the Earthkeeper was no longer granted while the building of a new temple took place. However, I do understand that there has been another ruling in the last year or so which allows anyone interested access to view the Earthkeeper.

A friend of mine returned recently from Kaua'i, very upset. Yes, she did 'view' the Earthkeeper, together with a vast number of people. Her sadness was due to the fact that she felt that the Earthkeeper appeared extremely low in energy and she did spend her entire visit meditating in its presence and giving it energy.

Miep and I had been extremely fortunate and were the only visitors on that occasion. We had been granted special permission to visit at a time when no visitors were allowed. While there, I naturally had to make the most of this special visit and spend as much time as possible in meditation within this crystal's special aura. I found its energy overpowering but was not entirely aware of the consequences of spending time in these very high vibrations! I did realise, however, that I could not stay in the temple for longer than ten to fifteen minutes at a time. So I interspersed it with walks in the beautiful garden in order to ground myself and chatted with the odd monk and a lovely lady caretaker. Towards the end of the day, during my last session, I managed to really link with this special being and was told this visit was just the beginning of my true crystal journey. How right she was!

Happily, and grateful for this wonderful experience, Miep and I resumed our three months' world trip. Little did I know of the intensive effect that day of the visit would have on me. It was a true healing crisis. From that day on, I would wake up every night at exactly 3 a.m., when I would be faced with, and worked through, an amazing emotional clearance programme. This lasted until the end of an otherwise lovely trip! Pictures from the past, all to do with clearing and forgiving, would pass through my mind during these hours in the night. It was like seeing these past events in a film, clear and often painful. It would often reduce me to tears and I had difficulty not to sob out loud as my sister Miep was enjoying a blissful, peaceful sleep. This review procedure would last until 5 am, by which time I would finally fall asleep, absolutely exhausted.

On my return home everybody expected me to be fully rested and recovered from my normally demanding life style. No so! I was ill for a fortnight after having dealt with all this emotional stuff night after night. On the positive side, I was aware of having gone through a healthy emotional cleanse and eventually felt all the better for it. Looking back, I realise that this was necessary. Realistically this was the only opportunity for me to go through this time-consuming cleansing process. In my everyday, far too busy life, it takes an effort to find time for meditation, let alone an in-depth clearing!

I am aware that it was the Earthkeeper's energy which set this event in motion and from that time onwards, my connection with crystals has taken a big leap forward. I felt impelled to talk about crystals and tell people about these wonderful beings. My poor friends must have thought me an interminable bore. Since I was already teaching other complementary therapies and was used to giving talks on these subjects, I expanded my repertoire to include 'crystals and their healing potential' and soon found that the request for 'crystal talks' exceeded all others. The next inevitable question from workshop attendants was, "When are you going to start teaching this subject?" Prospective students' were already lining up. It clearly was the Right Thing to do. As a consequence I started my school in 1992 and the students are still 'lining up'.

For me, another important event connecting with Earthkeepers came along in the mid-nineties. I regularly used to go to the wonderful Retreat Centre of the White Eagle Lodge in Montgomery, Texas, to give workshops on crystals and other therapies. It was there I met my friend Louise, who is not only involved with crystal beings, but is also an Earthkeeper enthusiast! It soon became an annual event for us both to drive to Arkansas where we visited various crystals mines. What could be a nicer holiday for two people who have an identical interest and love for crystals and especially the Crystal Earthkeepers?

Over the past years we had relied on finding little motels or other suitable accommodation en route, but this particular year, our friend Nancy joined us and we tried to find a suitable central point to stay during this trip rather than searching for a roof over our head every evening. Louise took this task upon her and came up trumps. She found us super accommodations where all kinds of wonderful workshops took place. It was a retreat centre in the beautiful countryside in the centre of Arkansas and, bliss of bliss, they actual supplied veggie food!

The moment we entered this peaceful place, we were bowled over by a most wonderful energy. Shirley, the owner, showed us around the amazing luxurious centre. As well as ample accommodation and space for workshops (one was going on at the time) there was a beautiful meditation room with very high energy. She informed us that the current group would gather there for a meditation at 8 am the next morning and we would be very welcome to join.

Shown to our luxurious room, my two mates settled down but I could not resist the pull of the incredible meditation room. I found an appropriate seat and settled in to meditate. It took only a few minutes to become aware of a strong energy coming up from the ground. On tuning in, I felt a familiar, exceptionally strong 'crystal energy' and soon realised there was a huge very special crystal below in the ground. I could see it in my mind's eye. At a guess it must have been twelve to fourteen feet high with one smaller, approximately six feet, growing out from the side. I did what every dedicated crystal lover would do, that is, sending it love and was surprised to get an immediate very strong energetic response. An avalanche of information came through, almost too much to remember.

In a nutshell, the crystal communicated that although people were aware that there was a big crystal in the ground, his Earthkeeper status was not known. Nevertheless, due to the meditations in this room he had been partially activated. Apparently he had been waiting for someone to recognise his presence and was literally 'rearing to go'. The difficulty was that in order for him to do so, he needed recognition, love and conscious dedication, so that he might take up his active role as Earthkeeper. Some ceremonies would have to be carried out to give him the opportunity to be properly activated, which would enable him to start his work. His instructions to me were to go to the owner of the centre and tell her this. In addition, there were various changes he wanted her to implement.

I was happy to be of help to him, but having arrived only a few hours ago, a newcomer to this place and a foreigner, I felt I could not really march off to this nice lady telling her what she ought to do! Somehow, that did not seem quite right.

Meantime, Louise too had spent some time meditating and also confirmed the presence of this large crystal that called himself an Earthkeeper.

It had been an amazing day, but it was not over yet; a lot more was yet to happen in this spiritual place....

After a delicious vegetarian meal that night, Louise, Nancy and I discussed the extraordinary happenings of the day in our room. Our hostess, bearing the comfort of her 'English' guest in mind, had pointed out how and where to make a decent cup of tea. She even had provided some Earl Grey from somewhere – bless her! This area was located in the large room that functioned both as dining room and workshop area, whatever the occasion required. It was a beautifully comfortable room and the tea-facility was alongside the wall immediately next to the entrance. Being thirsty after this extraordinary event, my friends sat down with a glass of iced tea (I have never been able to take to this adulteration of our national drink). My desire for a decent English cuppa was overwhelming, so I trotted off to the tea-making-facility in the big room.

On entering, I saw, to my amazement, a totally different interior! The luxury in the centre of the room had gone and it had changed to a Spartan look. There was a very large old-fashioned heavy wooden table and on the heavy wooden benches around it sat 9 Indians in ornate dress, complete with feathered headdresses. By the look of it they were having a meeting. They gave me some unwelcome looks, which made me feel very uncomfortable – I was clearly intruding. However my 'need' for a cup of tea was too strong. (Luckily the tea set-up on the wall table was still present). I therefore apologised for the interruption, explaining I would only be there for a few minutes to make a cup of tea and disappear. While waiting for the kettle to boil, my back was turned towards these unusual guests, but I felt extremely uncomfortable, aware they wanted me gone. However, one has one's priorities in life - in my case it was a decent cup of tea! Having made my cuppa, I once again apologised to the delegation and hastened back to our room.

Of course I was dying to tell Louise and Nancy what I had witnessed. Louise eager to see this, got up out of her chair to go and see for herself, but was in no uncertain way pushed back by an invisible hand and a strong voice saying NO! It was all rather exciting, and we chatted some more about this amazing place, and the day's events, and got ready for bed, but not before having decided to attend the early morning meditation with the visiting group.

On the way to the mediation room the next morning, I noted in passing that the main room had once again returned to its original comfortable state. The morning's mediation was a silent one. There must have been about fifteen to twenty people in attendance and the energy was incredible. I had barely relaxed when I became aware of the presence of 'my' crystal deep into the earth, energetically 'prodding' me. This was the moment he had been waiting for! His message to me was even more urgent than the previous day and came through very strong and clear with a, "You must tell her now". He took little or no notice of my silent protestations that this was not the ideal moment, but my new friend was determined. There was no likelihood I could meditate as I needed all of my energy to resist him. If you have never heard of a persistent crystal, you have now! The meditation became increasingly uncomfortable for me; I had to keep my eyes open, I fidgeted and tried hard not to relax, all the while enviously watching the devoted group deep in meditation. I counted the minutes....

Thank Goodness it was only a half - hour meditation. Everyone opened their eyes, looked relaxed and happy and said they had experienced a wonderful meditation. Lucky them!!

Shirley suddenly looked at me and asked how I had experienced the meditation in this special place as I had been raving about the lovely energies the previous day. As my mind was searching for some bland but true answer, Louise piped up: "Tell them, Lettie, about the crystal, what he wants and also what you saw last night". Well that was it! As I tried to formulate the entire experience, the Crystal had waited long enough. This was his chance to tell all. I have little recollection of what I said, but when I stopped everyone was gaping at me. The Crystal himself had made his wishes known.

To my amazement, Shirley did not seem too surprised and was delighted to know that there was a real-life Earthkeeper under her centre. It fitted in with the local history. The area in which this place had been built was known for its peaceful energies. We learned that the native Indians who used to live in this location had been known as healers and peacemakers. Whenever there would be a dispute between surrounding tribes the Elders would be invited to come to this spot. With their assistance and mediations on peace, differences were settled in this place. This explained the 'time/shift' scene I had observed the previous night.

The next day the owner of the centre, along with Nancy, Louise and me, spent the day buying crystals as 'ordered' by the Earthkeeper to create the right atmosphere in the meditation room and to help create the appropriate energy needed to start his activation. Once the crystals were dedicated and put in the right places special meditations were carried out, enabling this wonderful Earthkeeper to commence his active job and carry out his specific task.

THE EARTHKEEPERS NEED YOUR HELP

Although you may not have had the privilege of actually seeing an Earthkeeper, each one of you reading this book can contribute to their activation by sending them love and blessings in your regular meditations, or better still, you can hold a specific meditation to help these wonderful beings. You can either do this by yourself or as part of a group. The joint energy will have an even stronger effect.

Before you start your meditation it will help you to hold one of your favourite Quartz crystals in your right hand. The bond you already have with this crystal will facilitate your connection to the Earthkeepers and reinforce the energy that you send.

EARTHKEEPER MEDITATION

- Start by stating your intention, i.e. that this meditation is to help the right Earthkeeper in need of activation at this time. Trust that your love and energy will find the appropriate Earthkeeper. You may well get an impression about the Crystal Being chosen to be the recipient of your energies. This will help to make the experience more realistic for you.

- If you have seen your Earthkeeper in your mind's eye, visualise this particular crystal and surround it with light and love. Alternatively, you can simply visualise a huge quartz crystal or giant cluster knowing that this is a specific Earthkeeper.

- Then visualise this crystal being filled with a beautiful light. When it is completely saturated, see light rays coming from this crystal connecting with light rays from other Earthkeepers.

- Next visualise our precious planet and visualise the Earthkeepers as twelve major points of brilliant light, dotted all over our Mother Earth. It does not matter that you do not know their exact locations; your intent is sufficient to find them. See that all these Earthkeepers are now radiating and sending out the same rays of light as 'your' Earthkeeper. These rays connect and a strong grid of light is formed. Simultaneously, a multitude of smaller lights (minor Earthkeepers who connect to their big brothers or sisters) are radiating smaller beams. They all have the identical task of creating and forming a strong Web of Light to effect the healing of our planet and all its inhabitants; human, animal, plant and sea life.

- Hold this vision for a while and 'see' the positive healing of both Mother Earth and all life upon her accomplished.

- Finally, thank the Earthkeepers for their contribution towards restoring peace and harmony.

- In this meditation you are working on a spiritual level and it is therefore important to 'ground' yourself again. *(For details refer to the chapter on Meditation)*

On 'returning' from this meditation know that you have made a valuable contribution towards world healing by helping these crystal giants to create love, light and harmony.

This may appear a simple meditation, but it is very powerful, especially if many do this on a regular basis. It is a great and very effective way of working together with the Crystal Kingdom and a wonderful opportunity to help the Earthkeepers to carry out their contribution of restoring peace and harmony at this precious time in human history.

****

THE CRYSTAL SKULLS

Ever since I have been consciously aware of the existence of the crystal kingdom, I have read and heard about crystal skulls and been fascinated by them. My attention was finally drawn to them through one of those weird 'coincidences'. While visiting a colleague, whose life is dedicated to spreading the truth about crystal healing awareness, I met "Rainbow Man", an absolutely beautiful clear quartz crystal skull; he took my breath away. He was approximately 3½ x 4½ inches in size and was exquisite!

On questioning where he came from, I learned that she acquired him from a friend who had recently returned from South America and brought back several crystal skulls. When meeting this gentleman later and enquiring whether he had any more skulls for sale, he was rather cagey... (Peter truly loved his crystals and would not part with them except to the 'right person'.) He told me that during his trip in South America he came across a couple whose life's task was to fashion crystal skulls. These people said they had been instructed in meditation to make 13 and, at the time of his visit, this celestial task had just been completed. The couple at that time considered their mission finished, apart from distributing them to appropriate clients but, so they had been informed, this would be taken care of. Five skulls had already found their destination; one they would keep themselves, and the remaining seven were awaiting their 'pre-destined' homes. As I got to know Peter, I well understood how enamoured he had been with these beautifully fashioned crystal skulls and had wanted to buy all seven of them. Initially the couple would not consider it, but eventually became convinced that he was the person to find the 'right' homes for these exquisite skulls into which they had put so much, time, love and energy. Finally the day came when they allowed him to take these beautiful crystal skulls back home to the U.K. to their 'assigned' destinations.

When I met Peter there were only two crystal skulls left. The others had already found their chosen homes. Having seen the first one, I had literally fallen in love with it and was overcome by a strong desire to have one of these beautiful skulls. Having told this to my friend he mentioned he would consider it... After visiting my home and having assured himself that it was a suitable place, and I a suitable guardian for this one but last remaining assignment, I was allowed to purchase my precious little crystal skull. He also told me that he felt strongly that the people who had spent their lives carving these 13 crystals skulls, had done this in a previous life time, millennia or so ago. Thus, this beautiful Being entered my life and enriched it with his presence. It normally takes crystals a little while to settle in a new environment and this special little fellow was no exception, but when he did I was informed that he would like to be known as Gideon.... I was not surprised as crystals with a strong personality will often give me their name.

Crystal skulls have fascinated nearly everyone who has heard or read about them. Whenever the topic crops up, it usually causes a reaction, either positive or negative, but seldom indifferent! Somehow the subject of Crystal Skulls is shrouded in an air of mystery! People are curious and not sure what to make of it! Nevertheless, many people are interested and although reluctant to admit it, would like to know more! One explanation for this resistance could be because a skull does not exactly conjure up a pretty picture, or feelings of joy! It rather reminds us of our own mortality and the dreaded skull and bones! Not something we often want to dwell upon! - So why would people be fascinated by a crystal skull?

Much has been told and written about these wonderful crystal artefacts and eminent archaeologists, gemmologists and clairvoyants have suggested many theories about their origin and purpose. A great deal of scientific research has been carried out, and still continues today. Stories and legends abound, but through it all runs a common thread that hints at the fact that the original skulls were programmed a long, long time ago with ancient knowledge. We already know that crystals can retain a lot of information and although never written down, these stories were passed on verbally from generation to generation by many indigenous cultures all over the earth. In places where people honour Mother Earth and live close to nature these stories have been kept alive and they were, and still are, the ones with the ability to tune into crystals and nature.

To put you further into the picture, the story is simple and tells us that there are 13 special large ancient crystal skulls on our planet. These are located in various places around the globe, and some may probably still be in the earth. A tremendous amount of ancient wisdom is supposed to be stored collectively in these very special beings. According to an ancient legend all of these 13 skulls will one day be brought together. When this happens, they will divulge their combined wisdom, which will be of great importance and of immense benefit to mankind. Then we shall learn the true history of our planet and new information will be revealed to help heal; bring peace and harmony to suffering humanity; to animals; to Mother Earth and all forms of life upon her. All of this will happen at the appointed time. These skulls are ancient beings and, when considering preserving information, what better means would have survived the ravages of time, but quartz crystal? Today it is an accepted scientific fact that crystals can store a lot of information. We need look no further than the original silicon chip in our computers (Quartz crystal consists of Silicon Dioxide $SiO2$).

During the past century, several Crystal Skulls have already surfaced. Most of them are in the care of special people who know their value and importance and treat them with the respect they deserve. The best known is probably the Mitchell-Hedges skull. This is a beautifully clear and anatomically perfectly formed skull, as large as that of a small human being. This skull has a loose lower jaw and is known as the "talking skull". It acquired this name since it served as a channeller for much information passed on by respected mediums, who were able to establish a link with it.

This particular crystal skull was found in Belize in 1924 by Anna Mitchell-Hedges, who was accompanying her father Frederick Mitchell-Hedges on an archaeological dig in Belize. She tells the story of how, on the morning of her 17th birthday, she was wandering around the excavation site, and came upon the skull in an old temple. She noticed the sun glinting on something low down in the ruins. With the help of the archaeological party they retrieved it and to everybody's amazement it turned out to be a crystal skull. When it was shown to the local Mayan population, they were overjoyed and held great celebrations. As it was found on their home ground, the Mitchell-Hedges felt it was only right to donate the skull to the locals who greatly honoured and revered it.

During their three year stay in Belize, Frederick Mitchell-Hedges did much to help the local people in many ways and when he left, the villagers gave the skull to him in gratitude for the help he had given them. Initially the crystal skull was taken back to England but after Frederick died it has been cared for by his daughter Anna, who now lives in Canada.

As the fame of this precious artefact spread, Anna became aware that this crystal skull was very unique. Soon the scientific community, who were greatly intrigued by it, approached her. Where did it come from originally? How old was it? What was the purpose shaping a crystal in the form of a skull? How was it made?

One person with particular interest in the skull was the scientist Frank Dorland, who worked at the Hewlett-Packard laboratories in California. Hewlett-Packard is a well-known computer manufacturer, familiar with the properties of crystals. (After all the famous original silicon chip is quartz crystal...) He persuaded Anna to let him take the crystal skull to their laboratories for testing in an attempt to find answers to the many questions arisen.

Although the skull stayed within their laboratory for six years, many intriguing observations were made, but definite answers were not found. It had been impossible to ascertain how this crystal skull was crafted. The surface texture should give an insight into the type of instruments used to shape this skull, but when scrutinised under the electron microscope, there was nothing to indicate which types of instruments or implements could have been used to create it. To find a piece of pure clear quartz, large enough to fashion this skull, would have been extremely difficult and so the skull was tested for purity, (there are substances which very much look and feel like pure natural Quartz). The results however, proved without a doubt that this skull consists of pure natural quartz crystal, but the question of how it had been created remained a mystery. The same applies to the skull held in the British Museum; again after minute examination the results were inconclusive.

Theories abound as to the origin of these skulls. Some believe that they have come from another dimension and brought within them much wisdom, or were fashioned by earlier highly advanced civilisations and programmed with their technology. Others believe they are a man-made hoax. Whatever their origin, to date the answer is indecisive.

In my opinion the skulls are ancient databases. Bearing in mind the importance of passing on the advanced knowledge of the time by the wise ones of possibly Atlantis, or Egypt, to future generations, crystal would have been an obvious choice. The very fact that crystals can record and contain information, what could be a more logical object for storing knowledge for future mankind than the image/object of a human brain, in this case a 'crystal' brain. These artefacts would keep knowledge in custody for generations to come, safeguarding the information regardless of the ravages the earth might endure. Crystal skulls, which could store this knowledge in condensed form, were ideal receptacles. With forethought, the ancient wise ones knew that, at an appropriate time in the future, humanity would once again awaken to greater spiritual and technical understanding and there would be a need for their knowledge to re-emerge. Enlightened souls would be in a position to access the wisdom stored within these skulls and they would be able to pass on and apply the advanced knowledge and technology once again.

We tend to think of ancient inhabitants of the earth as 'simple', yet are gradually discovering that nothing is more off the mark than this assumption. Just take a look at the pyramids of Egypt and the immense know-how and precision required building them! Even today, with all our scientific knowledge, it still leaves the most eminent architects puzzling about the way they were built. Take a look at the South American cities recently rediscovered and the amazing artefacts found there. This is hardly the work of simpletons!

Dorland is of the opinion that crystal skulls are in fact ancient computers, containing a vast amount of information, which is at present not accessible to all humans. However due to the present influx of higher frequencies that continue to bombard our Mother Earth and all of us living on it, the energies of our physical bodies are in the process of becoming more sensitive. This should in due course facilitate communication with subtler life forms, including the information stored in these crystal beings and, when that time comes, much will be learned. Dorland is of the opinion that the human body, as well as Quartz crystal, continuously sends out additional electro magnetic waves on a frequency not yet audible to most of us. As we evolve, this will gradually become a conscious part of us, opening an entirely new source of communication and, consequently, information.

The transformative aspect of crystals, including the potential of working with crystal skulls (whatever their size), is often overlooked. They can teach us a lot and help us with our personal evolution.

As an individual to learn and feel comfortable when working with a crystal skull involves a personal confrontation with oneself. It means having to face and accept one's greatest subconscious fears and makes us look at the shadow side of ourselves. Meditating with skulls can be a truly transformative experience, but once a breakthrough has been achieved, it opens up the way to receiving insight on fundamental truths. The initial experience may be somewhat uncomfortable, but it can help us achieve the healing and clarity we need in this, the 21st century.

****

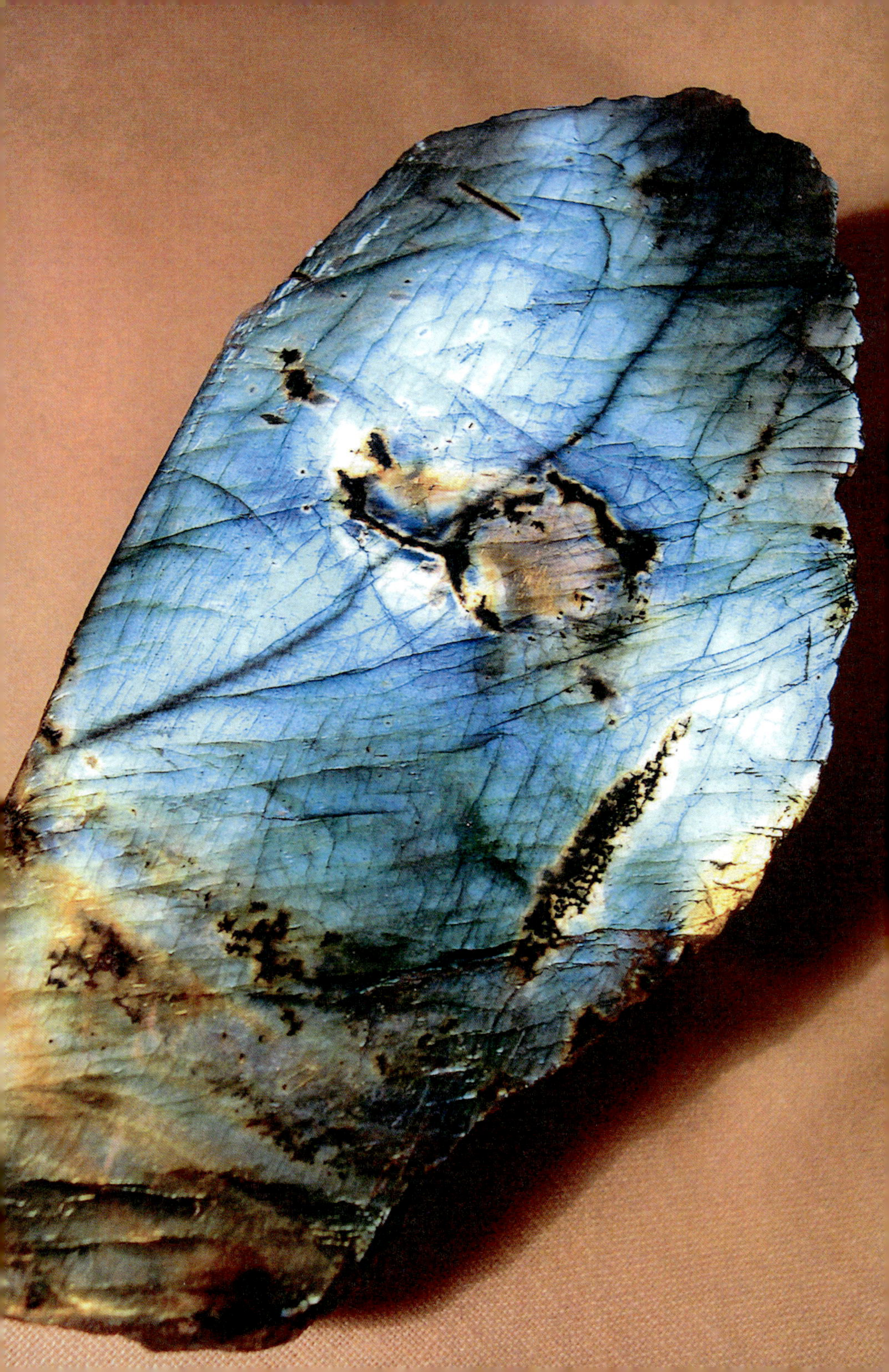

Labradorite

EXPOSE YOUR SENSES TO CRYSTAL THERAPY

EXPOSE YOUR SENSES TO CRYSTAL THERAPY

Locating a Qualified Therapist

If you have never experienced a crystal healing session, you may well be tempted to try it after reading this book. Great decision! The obvious thing to do first is to find a suitably qualified therapist in your vicinity. By the way, whatever therapy you go for, it is important to find someone with appropriate qualifications. This is particularly important when you decide to have a crystal healing treatment. You will already have gathered from the contents and information in this book that crystals are extremely powerful tools and it is therefore of the greatest importance that you choose your therapist with considerable care. - So, how to go about this?

By now you have already decided to look for a properly qualified crystal therapist with at least two years of training under their belt. This time period is an essential part of the training to develop the sensitivity, intuition skills and intimate knowledge of a vast number of healing crystals, as well as knowledge of the physical and subtle bodies. The properly qualified professional crystal therapist has completed a minimum training of two years at an accredited college.

There are many bona fide colleges in the U.K. and elsewhere in

Europe teaching to high standards of crystal healing. The principals and teachers of these colleges are very aware and concerned of the potential hazards caused by people setting up practice after attending a 'quickie' course. It is with this in mind that responsible colleges/schools want to create public awareness of their 'options'. To give an example let us see what has been happening in the U.K.

In Great Britain there are two recognised main umbrella organisations in the crystal therapy field, i.e. CHF (Crystal & Healing Federation) and ACHO (Association of Crystal Healing Organisations). Both organisations work to the highest standards teaching crystal therapy. Aware of the need to set proper standards, both organisations got together to set the highest national standards and formed the BCH (British Crystal Healers). This now is the largest crystal healing organisation in the U.K. and the standards set by the BCH are of the highest order.

There are several ways in which you can locate a BCH qualified therapist in your area, and the simplest option is to get on to the internet and log in to the BCH, the CHF or ACHO website. (Details can be found on the reference page of this book) Alternatively, you can phone the CHF or ACHO for further information. As a potential client and armed with this knowledge you can feel safe when treated by crystal therapists whose qualifications confirm their membership to the above organisations. When you make an appointment with a crystal therapist do not be afraid to ask for their qualifications and to which professional organisation they belong. The bona fide therapist will be happy to supply this information.

What to Expect During a Crystal Healing Session

Since there are many schools and colleges teaching crystal healing, some minor differences exist in the way crystal treatments are applied, but the fundamental principles are the same and as long as you ensure your therapist belongs to the CHF or ACHO you know you are in safe hands. To give you an outline of what to expect when you have a crystal therapy session, I set out below what you would experience if you went to a therapist trained by the Vantol College.

When you phone for an appointment, your therapist will ask you some questions during the conversation to ascertain if crystal therapy is beneficial for you. As with other therapies there are certain contra-indications,[13] which means that this might not be the ideal therapy for your specific health condition. Obviously it is important for the therapist to find this out before giving you a treatment.

Also to be taken into account, is the fact that crystal healing is an energy treatment, unlike other 'hands-on' treatments. Bearing this in mind the therapist will ask you to wear natural clothing for the session, such as cotton, linen, wool or silk. The reason for this is that energy does not move easily through artificial fibre, which would obstruct the healing energy passing through your clothing. And if you are a lady, you may also be asked to refrain from applying perfume as this affects one's aura and makes it difficult for the therapist to assess the real state of your energy field.

In order to give you the best possible treatment, your therapist will ask you some more questions on arrival to help her/him to assess the best possible treatment for you. She/he will also explain exactly what to expect during the session and answer any questions you may have about the treatment. You will be asked to take off your shoes (no undressing) and take off your watch and any jewellery during the treatment. The reason for this is that the energy of crystals has been known to upset the delicate time keeping of quartz watches. With regard to jewellery, we do not always think of our beautiful gems, decorating our rings, pendants and earrings as crystals, but that is exactly what they are. They are in fact the most superior quality of crystals, i.e. gem quality. Though these precious stones are healers themselves, the therapist wants to apply the crystal energy you need at that moment to the exclusion of other energies, however nice they may be. Since many clients enjoy soothing music during the session, you may also be asked if you

[13]   A contra-indication is a health condition which might adversely affect the client if she were to receive this therapy.

would like some gentle music or prefer the silence.

Having dealt with all these preliminaries it is time to lay down on the couch and simply relax. Your therapist will make you as comfortable as possible so that you may fully enjoy the treatment. During the session the therapist will place crystals around you and some on you. At some stage she may touch your head and/or your feet, but she will mainly work in your energy field. During the session most clients experience a feeling of well-being and often have a sense of being wrapped in a warm blanket. Many people are so relaxed that they fall asleep, only to wake up at the end of the session with a beautifully rested and feel-good feeling.

As you are very relaxed after the session, you may have the feeling that you would like to remain in that blissful state… However, it is time to return to your everyday world, expectantly with more energy and a peaceful mind. After absorbing the healing energy during the treatment it is possible that you feel slightly light-headed, but your therapist will be aware of this and take action to ensure that you really have both feet on the ground before you leave the premises. She/he will gently help you to get up and 'ground you', bringing you back to a state of 'worldly awareness' You are usually offered a drink of water while your therapist discusses your treatment with you and once again ensure that you are thoroughly grounded before going home.

THE EFFECTS OF A CRYSTAL THERAPY TREATMENT

Each treatment is different since it is geared to the client's individual energetic needs, but the outcome of the treatment is the proof in the proverbial 'pudding'. To give you an idea what and how clients feel after a treatment, the following remarks by clients may give you an insight:

- "I feel very relaxed."
- "You have taken a heaviness off me"
- "I feel lighter"

- "I feel more positive!"
- "My depression has lifted"
- " I feel more energetic"
- " I feel strong and can cope again"
- "I feel so calm and peaceful"

On the odd occasion a client may not feel a strong benefit immediately, but when this is the case the client invariably phones her therapist the next day or so, to say how very much better she is. The reason for this is that many energy adjustments have taken place in the body during the treatment and the body takes time to adjust to these changes. Once this has taken place and harmony has been re-established, the client will feel the beneficial effects of the treatment.

The best way to find out what a crystal treatment can do for you is to find the Right Therapist (properly accredited!) and treat yourself to a session. Remember, you do not necessarily have to have a health condition to benefit from a treatment. It does wonders for your body, emotions and morale and who does not need that in these stressful times! I have one 'regular' who comes for what she calls her body's M.O.T. and would not miss it for the world!

****

BIBLIOGRAPHY

Vibrational Medicine - Dr. Richard Gerber, Bear & Co., Santa Fe, N.Mexico,
ISBN 1-879181-28-2

Crystal Power Crystal Healing - Michael Gienger, 1998, Blandford. Lndon

The Curious Lore of Precious Crystals – George Fredrick Kunz, 1913, General Publishing Co.Ltd,, Toronto. Ont. Canada.
ISBN 0-486-22227-6

Gifts of the Gemstone Guardians - Michael Katz – Golden Age Institute.
ISBN 0-92470-75-0 – Portland, Oregan

Crystals & Healing for Everyone – Henriette Maasdijk -
ISBN 0-9547569-0-8

Crystal Enlightenment, - , Katrina Raphaell ISBN 0-943358-27-2;
Crystal Healing , Katrina Raphaell ISBN 0-943358-30-2 and
The Crystallline Transmission – Katrina Raphaell - ISBN 0943358-33-7
Aurora Press, New York

Holly Ice, Frank Dorland (Galde Press, Phyllis Galde, P.O. Box 65611, St.Paul - MN 55165. - ISBN 1-880090-02-3

Crystals, the Science, Mysteries & Lore - Douglas Bullis – Crescent Books, New York 1990 - ISBN 0-517-68929-4

The Magic of Precious Stones. - Mellie Uyldert –The Aquaran Press 1981, ISBN 9-780850-307986

The magic & Science of Jewels & Stones - Isidore Kozminsky, Cassandra Press 1989 ISBN 0-9615875

Mysteries of the Crystal Skulls Revealed - Sandra Bowen, Nocerina and Shapiro Thorsons, London – ISBN 0-7225-3485-X

The Message of the Crystal Skull, - Alice Bryant & Phyllis Galde Llewellyn Publishing, P.O. Box 64383-092, St.Paul, MN 55164-0383

Igniting Soul Fire, Spiritual Dimensions of the Bach Flower Remedies - Gay Mack, Polair Publishing, London, 2004. ISBN 0-9545389

Gem Elixirs & Vibrational Healing, Gurudas, Cassandra Press 1989, ISBN 0-961-58750-4

Roman Book on Precious Stones, Sydney H.Ball, Gemological Institute of America 1950

Die Heilsteine der Hildegard von Bingen - Anja & Michael Gienger - Neue Erde Verlag, Saarbrücken, Germany. ISBN 3-89060-224-X

USEFUL ADDRESSES

Lettie
Vantol College of Crystal Therapy
11 Heather Close
Addlestone, Surrey
KT15 3PF
E-mail: info@vantolcollege.co.uk
www.vantolcollege.co.uk 01932 423696

Vibrational Healing Foundation
6 Buer Road
London
SW6 4LA
E-mail: VHFLondon@aol.co
www.vibrationalhealingfoundation.co.uk

CHF (Crystal & Healing Federation)
6 Buer Road
London. SW6 4LA
www.crystalandhealing.com

BCH (British Crystal Healers)
www.britishcrystalhealers.org

E-mail info@britishcrystalhealers.org

CMA (Complementary Medical Association)
www.the-cma.org.uk

Flower Essences are available by post from:
Healing Herbs
P.O.Box 65
HEREFORD
HR2 0UW
www: healingherbs.co.uk